Welcome to the eighth in my ongoing series of booklets introducing you to contempo their craft. Through these booklets you will meet some of the best and most inter beadmakers. You will learn more about them and their work. They will take this op their beadmaking secrets.

These booklets serve as companion documents to my text, **More Than You Ever Wanted To Know About Glass Beadmaking**. That text provides the basic knowledge of glass beadmaking skills while these booklets will show you how different artists put these skills into practice. In these adventures into beadmaking, I will assume that you have a passing knowledge of glass beadmaking techniques and will not try to go into all the basics of the craft. Instead, we will focus on how these beadmakers work their wonders.

For this booklet, I have chosen to give you a glimpse into the work of another of my favorite beadmaking artists, Diana East. I first met Diana East at the 2002 Gathering in Alexandria, VA where I, like everyone else, was impressed by her Aladdin's Palace presentation. The images that she was creating were without compare. I am sure that you too will be enthusiastic about her work and the new playful direction that it has taken.

Artist Bio

Diana lives in Enderby, Great Britain with her husband Dave. She got her degree in interior design and worked for a number of years as a museum gallery designer. From there she tried her hand as a jeweler and loved the artistic process, but hated doing commissions. She then spent a few years as a showroom manager and product tester for an arts and crafts material supplier for schools. It was there, while working with every other form of craft that her interest in glass was born. It was while helping the company expand its craft line into mosaic glass and getting the chance to play with glass that her fascination for melting it on a small scale began.

Diana had searched all over Britain trying to find information on shaping glass for her jewelry. She knew that it could be done because she had found a catalogue from the 1993 Gathering. She was told that she would have to go to America to learn more. Then in 1996 she, along with the rest of the British glass art scene, was awakened to the potential of glass beadmaking by an article in *Country Living* magazine about glass bead artist Heather Bellman. Diana was soon able to weasel her way as a helper into a class being taught by an American beadmaker at the home of a British bead society member. The teacher was none other than Kate Drew-Wilkinson, the aunt who had taught Heather Bellman. She and Kate hit it off so well that by the end of the class, Kate invited Diana to come to America and stay with her.

So Diana trundled off to America where she had an incredible experience working with Kate for two months, but worked herself to the point of exhaustion and ended up getting sick. Diana has suffered from chronic fatigue syndrome for years, ever since giving birth to her daughter Lucy, and because of it she can need months to recover from an illness. This was a trying time for Diana because so much else was going on in her life. She had to sell her house and move her daughter into her own flat, but her loving husband nursed her through it.

Chain Reaction and Loop, 2004
Photo by: the artist

Diana, now convinced that she wanted to work in glass but thinking she wanted to work on a larger scale, studied for a year at the International Glass Centre where she learned a lot about glass. She followed this with residencies at DeMonfort University and University of Central England, and a post-graduate class at Derby University. Then in May 2001, while pushing herself at the physically demanding task of glassblowing from a furnace in preparation for an exhibition, she had another partial collapse.

She is convinced that part of reason for this collapse was that her body was trying to tell her that she should work on small things like beads. She had been resisting it because she knew the prejudices of the art world where beadmaking was considered frivolous, more of a craft than a real art form.

So she lived a schizophrenic life for a while trying to be both a beadmaker and a glassblower. She was experimenting with all sorts of techniques and applying them in interesting ways to her beads, but was not feeling fulfilled. She considers much of her work – her Ancient, Monet, Klimpt, Wave, Ruins, Aladdin Palace, Mosque, and Cityscape designs – derivative and just copies of other art pieces, although in a different media. They all sold well and provided plenty of technical challenge without the punishing physical labor, but did not fulfill the need for art and originality that the "artist" inside her demanded.

Diana has finally addressed this challenge in her new work by basing it on reading that she has done in science. She is fascinated by the unexpected vagaries of quantum physics and the fantastic structures of neuroscience, and how the two may combine somehow down at the smallest levels to produce such a chaotic phenomena as consciousness. She finds it a mystical, strange realm which boggles the minds of lay people and scientists alike. The biological structure of the brain with its many interconnections and electrochemical impulses has inspired her new work. She tries to artistically represent how these processes take place in ones nerves and mind. This representation will be most apparent in my discussion of her Little Thinker Bead which is her artistic expression of the dynamic process of thought on the molecular level.

She has followed this theme of thought and consciousness to the macroscopic level investigating the metaprograms recorded in the brain and resulting reactions on the interactions between people. This concept of social interactions and reactions was the basis for an exhibition in Holland called "What's Up."

Diana was also influenced somewhat by science fiction and how it relates to this theme. She was fascinated by the movie, *The Matrix*, with its dual nature of reality, one underlying the other, and the image of the computer code flowing down the monitor screen. She used the concept and the image as the springboard for the developing her Thought River Series with its very different inner and outer appearances.

Diana is in the forefront of the British bead movement, helping it to define itself and to gain acceptance in the art world at large. She is participating on a committee of the Contemporary Glass Society, the British equivalent of the U.S.-based Glass Art Society, to which she also belongs, trying to help break down the boundaries between sculptural and bead art. She is setting up a workshop on flameworking, fusing, and pâte de verre for the Contemporary Glass Society to be held in May 2005.

Skyscraper Bead, 2001
Photo by: the artist

Mosque Bead, 2001
Photo by: the artist

Birches Bead, 2001
Photo by: the artist

Trees Bead, 2001
Photo by: the artist

Aladdin's Palace Bead, 2001
Photo by: the artist

Moonlit Ruins Bead 2001
Photo by: the artist

Above: Ringed Bead, 2002
Right: Pod Bead, 2002
Photos by: the artist

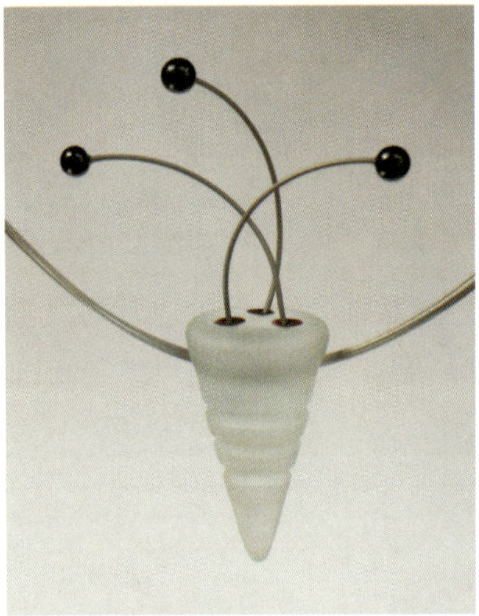

Left:
Exocytosis Bead, 2004
Photo by: the artist

Right:
Sodium Spike, Action Potential Bead, 2004
Photo by: the artist

Below & Left: Stripe Over Stripes Beads, 2003 Photos by: the artist
Below Right: Random Stripe Bead, 2002 Photo by: the artist

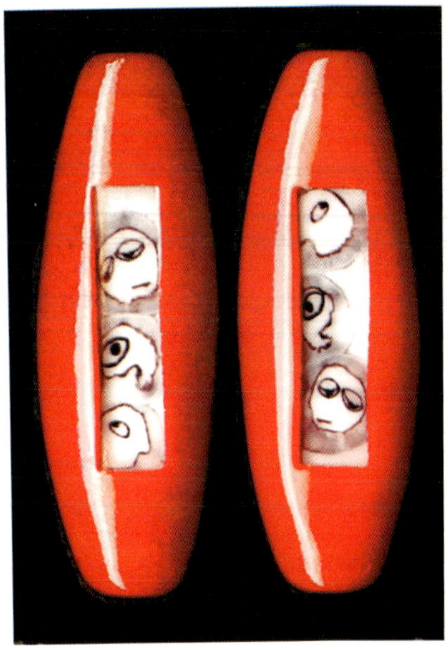

Left:
Family Entertainment Beads, 2003
Photo by: the artist

Right:
Compartment Beads, 2003
Photo by: the artist

Below:
Who's Looking Bead, 2003
Photo by: the artist

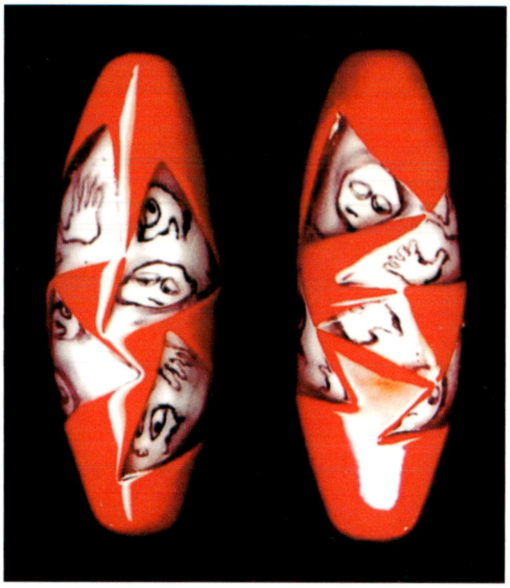

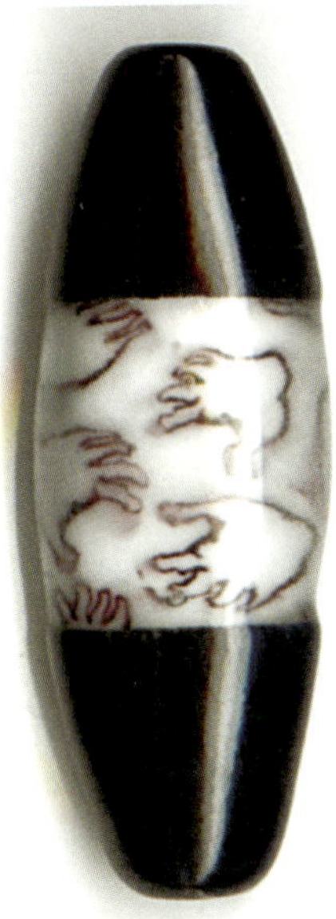

Above Left: Hand It To You Bead, 2003

Above Right: Family Entertainment, 2003
"It's Easy to Get Drawn into an Argument"

Above Center and Below: Beads from the "What's Up" exhibition in Holland, 2003

Photos by: the artist

(Someone Knows More Than He Is Letting On)

Toxic Thoughts, 2004
Photo by: the artist

Action Potential, 2004
Photo by: the artist

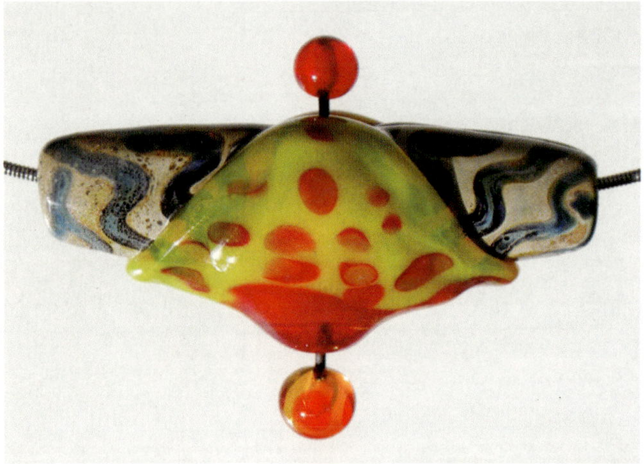

Yellow Mantle, 2004
Photo by: the artist

Expectation, 2004
Photo by: the artist

Brain Fever, 2004
Photo by: the artist

Thought Pattern, 2004
Photo by: the artist

Wave Bead

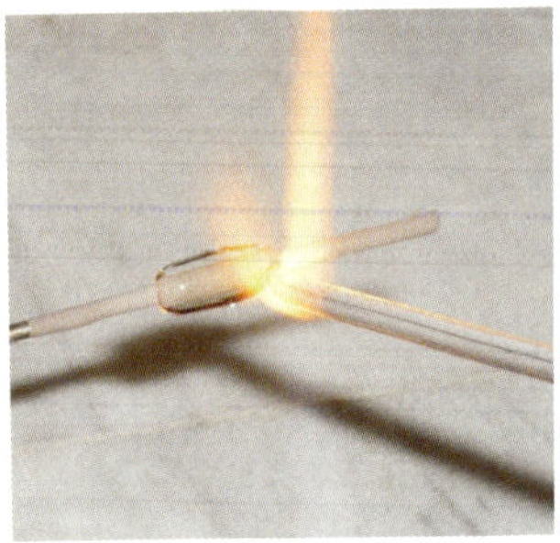

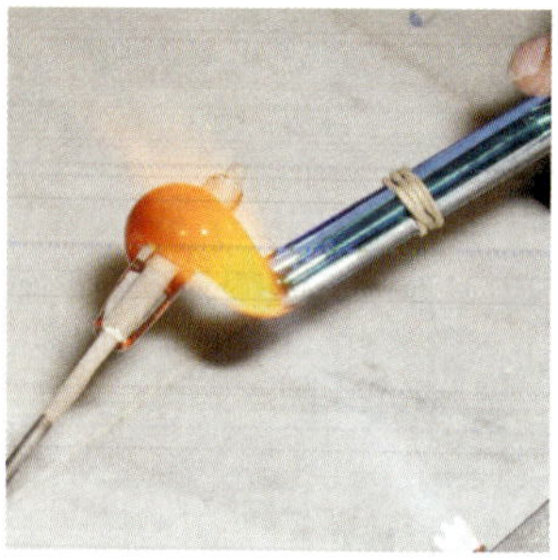

For the first demonstration in this booklet Diana makes a fun bead that she calls her wave bead. She calls it this because it looks like a wave breaking over the bead and incorporates the idea of neural waves enveloping the bead.

Diana starts by winding a long clear bicone bead, as on the left side of the page. In the first two photos we see her winding the glass onto the mandrel. She applies the glass relatively hot so that it is completely molten and flows smoothly. She keeps slight pressure against the glass already in place on the mandrel, almost mixing the current and the previous wraps together. This minimizes any trapping of air at this interface resulting in a nice clear bead. After she has applied all the clear glass she needs to the mandrel and has the general shape that she wants, Diana goes back and finishes the bicone shape to better define the ends. She does this by heating the first end, as in the center left photo, and then rolling the end on her paddle, as in the fourth photo on the left. She then repeats this process on the other end of the bead.

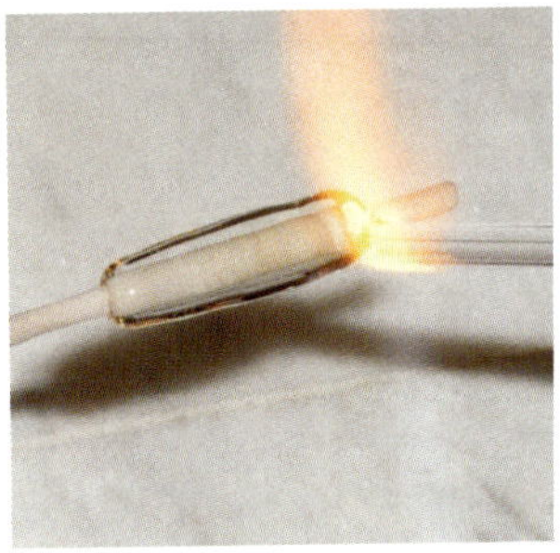

Now Diana applies a thick wrap of hot glass that she will randomly deform in the next step of the process. She does this by developing a large multicolored gather on the end of a cluster of three rods, as in the lower left photo. For this example she is using one rod of transparent turquoise and two rods of medium transparent blue. When she develops a large enough gather, she superheats it to the point where she can just barely keep it balanced on the end of the rod cluster and then quickly wraps the glass around the center of the bead, as in the upper right photo.

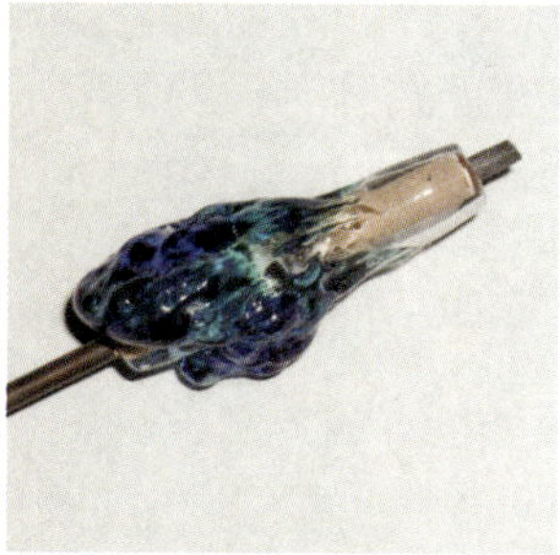

Next comes the random step. Diana immediately plunges the bead into a cup of perlite to deform the molten glass into a wave, as in the second photo on the right. The resulting deformation depends on a number of variables. First, the heat of the glass determines how easily it flows. Second, the material's hardness affects how much it can push against the glass. She uses perlite or vermiculite because it is soft and resistant to the heat of the glass. Third how fast and hard she pushes the bead into the cup affects how the glass deforms. Last, the direction she enters into the material will affect the direction the glass moves. With a cup you can only push directly into the media, but with a bowl you can push almost perpendicular to the bead axis. After this step the molten glass is pushed over to one side and the granularity of the perlite puts all sorts of dimples into its surface, as in the center right photo. The bead is then annealed in a kiln.

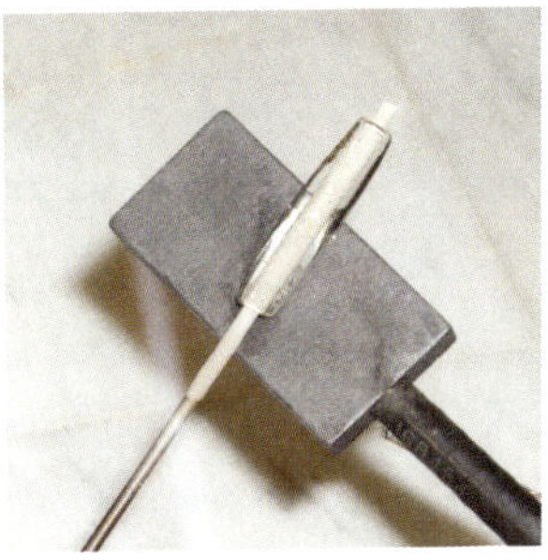

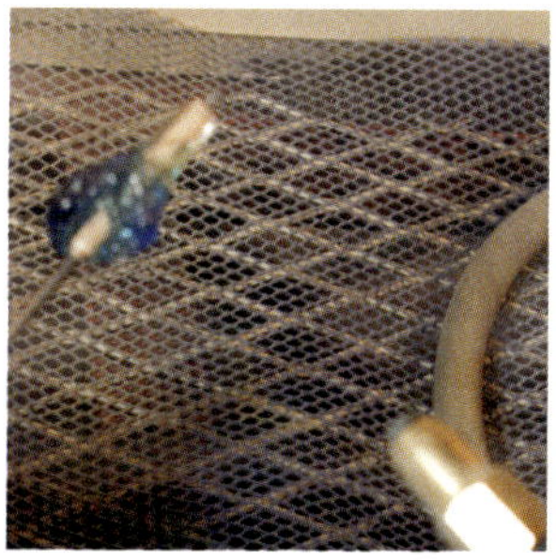

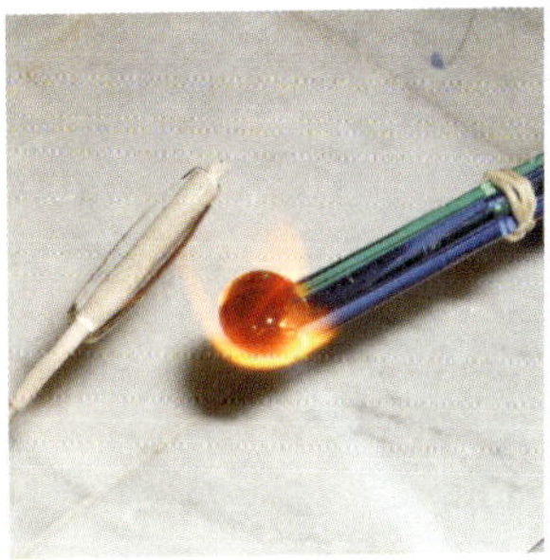

Since Diana likes a matt finish on many of her beads she decides to sandblast the bead, as she is doing in the fourth photo on the right. It also helps remove traces of the perlite. We will discuss more about sandblasting later. The finished bead can be seen in the lower right photo.

Using Powdered Enamels

Diana uses a lot of enamels in her work to achieve two basic effects. First, she puts thin coatings on beads that she can cut, polish, or blast through to expose parts of the bead beneath. Second, she likes to use enamels to get the kind of color variation on a bead surface that she would not be able achieve any other way. The enamels that she uses are the 9000 series of Thompson enamels that are made to be compatible with Effetre glass. The enamel colors that are available can be seen in the photo to the left. This bead color pallet was put together by Kate Fowle Meleney, who encouraged and worked with Thompson Enamels in developing the 9000 series.

The enamels are finely ground colored glass that has been formulated to have the same 104 coefficient of expansion (COE) as Effetre glass, as well as being highly fluxed so that it is softer, i.e. melts at a lower temperature, and will flow easily on the surface of a bead.

To apply enamel on glass, the glass is heated so that the enamel will stick, the enamel is applied to the glass, and the glass is reheated to melt the softer enamel and allow it to flow on the bead surface. You can achieve a spotty application or a continuous layer by controlling where you heat the bead before sprinkling on the enamel. How hot you reheat the bead will determine whether you get a pebbly or a smooth surface. The enamels are applied by rolling the glass in them or by sprinkling them onto the glass surface. The tools that are typically used to sprinkle enamels onto a bead are small screened baskets like those seen to the left. These sifters come in three sizes; ½", 1¼" and 2" diameter. The enamel is shaken out of the sifter by running your fingernail up and down the spiral wound wire handle. For best results the sifter should not be more than half full. Diana, on the other hand uses a set of vials, like spice jars with screens mounted in the top, as in the lower right photo. She got them from Creative Glass in Switzerland, and uses them to sprinkle enamels onto her beads. Whenever she wants to apply enamel to a bead she sprinkles it on using the vials like salt shakers.

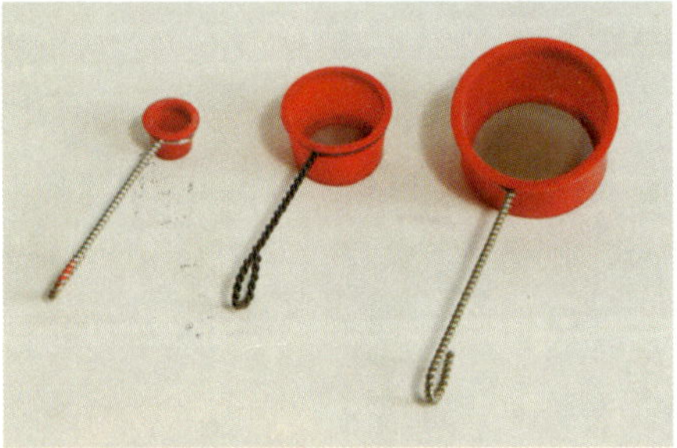

Since a lot of the enamel does not stick as she shakes it onto the bead, Diana catches the excess on pieces of paper, labeled for each color, that she positions below the bead. Then after the bead is done she can pour the excess enamel on each piece of paper back into the appropriate vial.

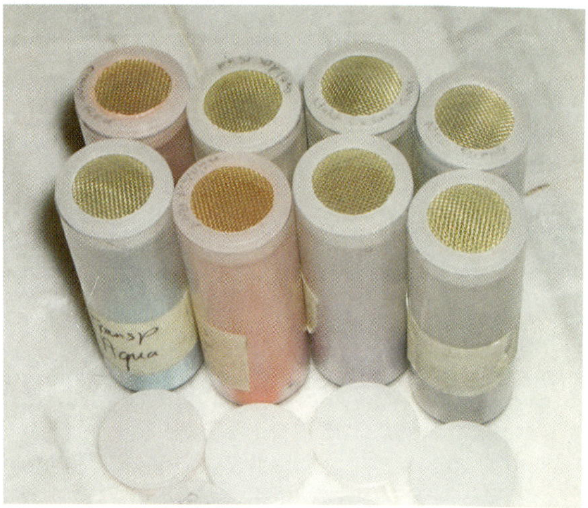

Whenever you use glass powders and enamels you need to be aware of safety concerns with their use. They are typically loaded with heavy metals that can cause chronic problems. To avoid inhaling them, I would recommend having a good ventilation system and wearing a good particulate respirator. To avoid ingesting them, adopt good work practices including wet clean up of any spills, washing your hands after use, and no eating, drinking or smoking in the work place.

Family Interactions Bead

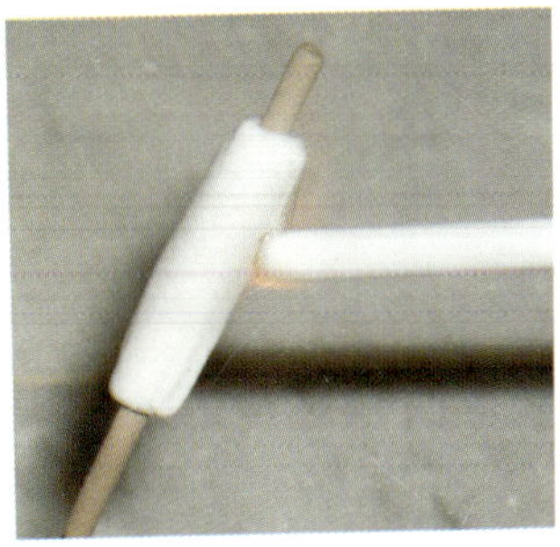

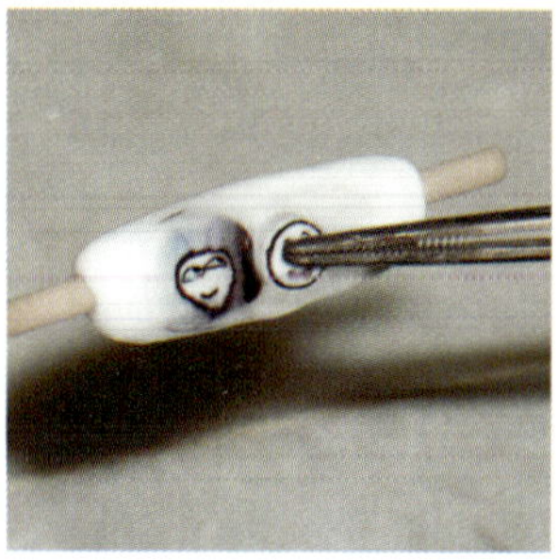

This bead is part of Diana's series on human interactions. In this case it represents the interactions within a family unit, the members of which are represented by the three face canes. I could easily see it as the interactions in my own family with the two monkeys in my life, my wife and my son (their Chinese astrological birth signs), playing pranks on me, the serious tiger in the center.

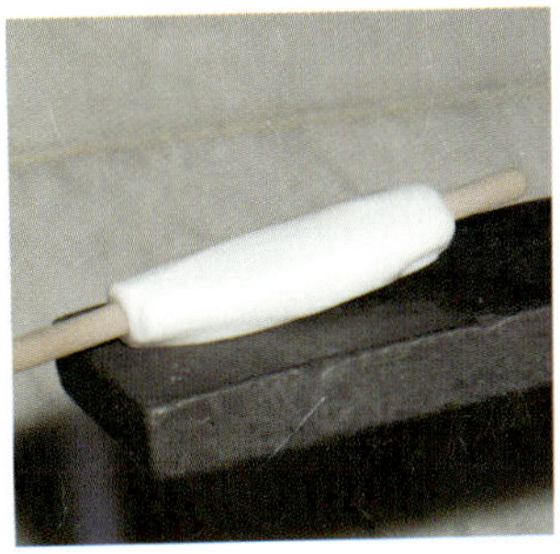

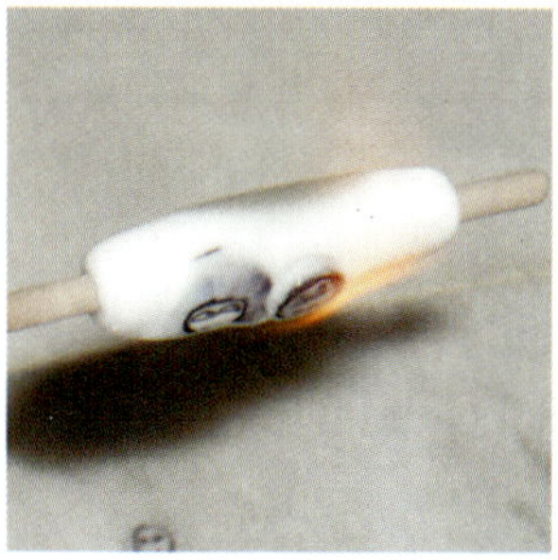

Diana starts this bead with a short cylindrical white base to which she adds stripes of more white along one side to make it a little wider there, as in the upper left photo. This is a work style that I have not seen before. Diana will often wind on her first layer of glass and then rough shape the bead by adding succeeding layers of glass by painting them on axially. Next, she smoothes the bead into shape using the heat of the flame and pressure from her paddle, as in the second photo on the left. She chose white as the color for the base bead because it is the color that she used for the background in her face canes.

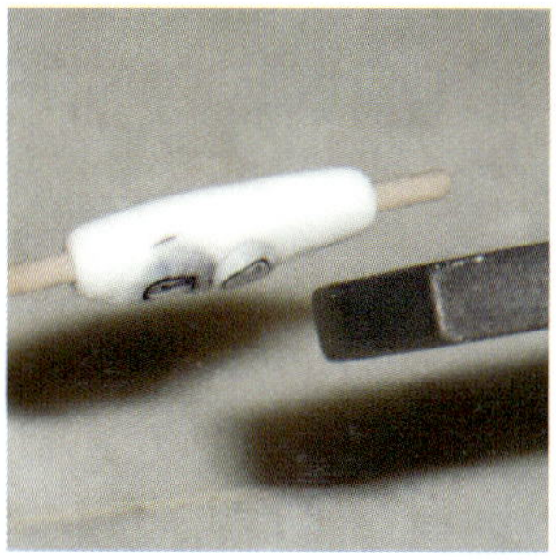

The center left photo shows the three face cane chips that Diana is going to embed into the side of this bead. To learn how to make these simple face canes see Diana's article on the process in the October 2004 bead issue of Lapidary Journal or the chapter on figurative cane construction in my beadmaking book. The fourth photo on the left shows the first face chip installed in place on the left side of the bead. Notice that Diana is getting bleeding of the black glass in the cane onto the bead surface as she installs the chips. This can be avoided, if desired, by grinding the chips thinner.

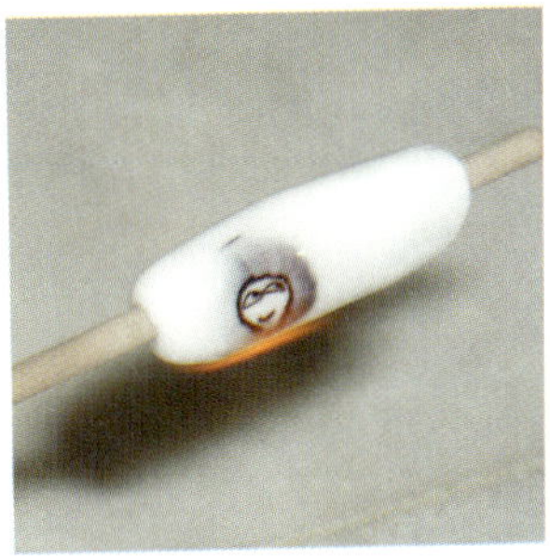

The next five photos show the process that Diana goes through to install each of these chips. In the lower left photo she is warming the chip in the side of her flame and is locally heating the application point on the bead. When the white glass at the application point starts to turn clear, she applies the chip and then immediately pushes on it with the back of her tweezers, as in the upper right photo. But as is usually the case, it does not go in all the way and further work is required to push it into the surface.

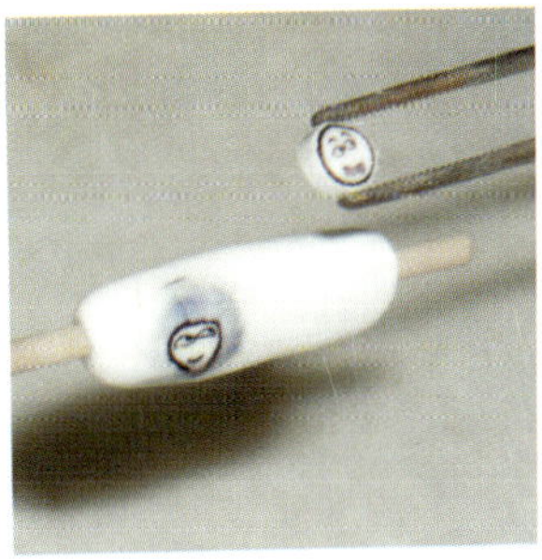

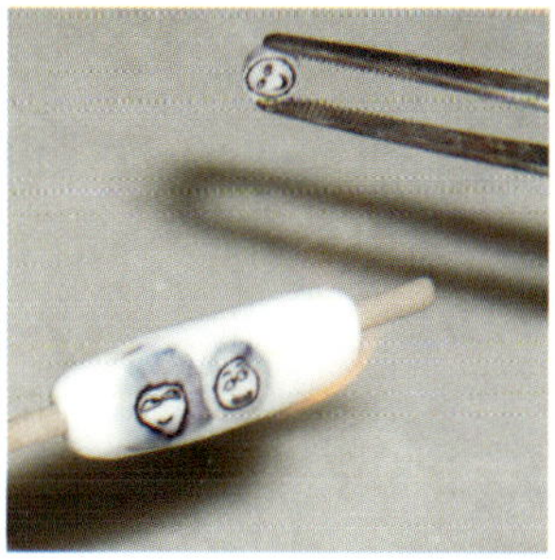

The steps for working the chip into the bead amount to heating the chip-bead interface, as in the second photo on the left. Heating of the front and back of the bead is followed by pushing the chip in with her paddle, as in the center right photo. Before pushing too hard on the chip with the paddle, she lets the paddle rest gently on the exposed chip surface to chill it and then applies pressure straight down to push it into the bead, which is still fluid. This procedure prevents the chip from smearing or expanding in size as she pushes.

She finishes the application process by lightly heating the bead surface and smoothing out the edge of the chip, as in the fourth photo on the right. She then repeats the process on the last chip, as she is starting to do in the lower right

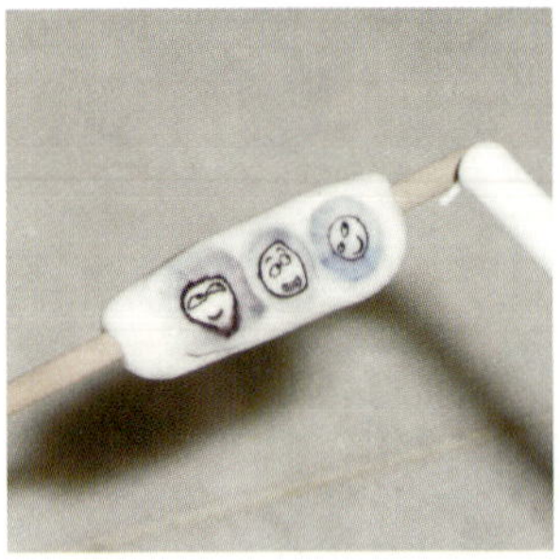
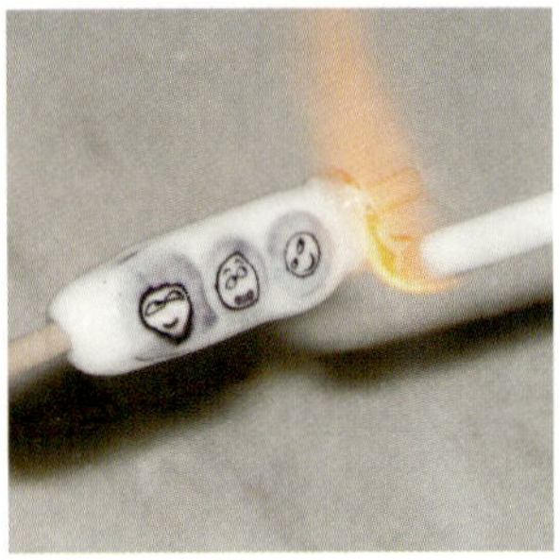
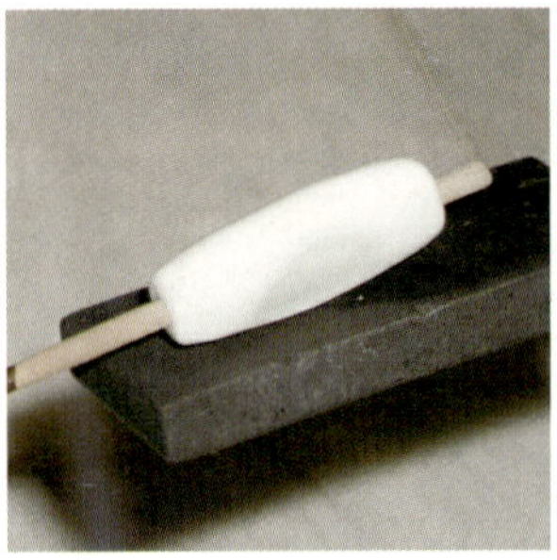
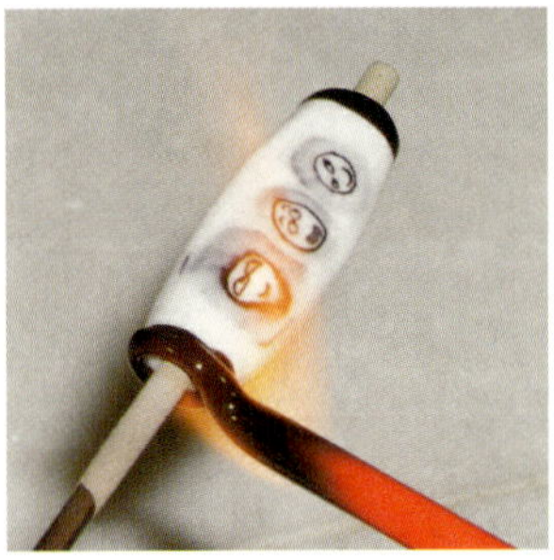
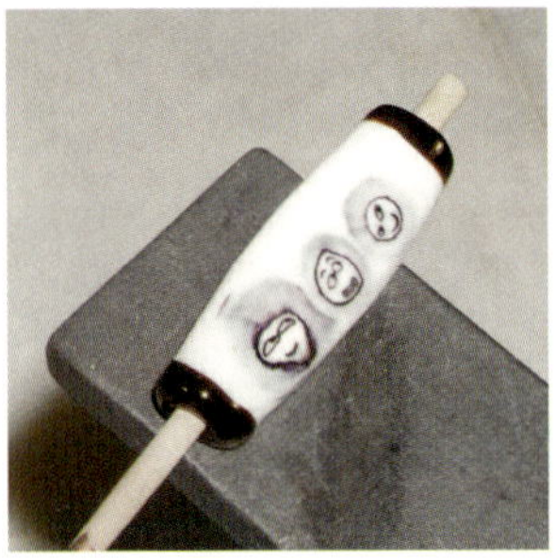

photo. The photo to the upper left shows the three chips worked into the surface of the bead.

During installation of a figurative cane chip into a bead, the shape of the bead can often be distorted by the pressure to apply the chip. For this reason, Diana's next step will be to redefine the bead shape. This is what she is doing in the next two photos on this page. In the second photo on the left she is applying additional white glass to the right end of the bead. This glass will rebuild the smooth flattened bicone shape that was distorted during addition of the last chip. This additional glass will also balance out the white background on the bead with equal lengths on either side of the family. In the center left photo she is shaping the glass and the rest of the bead into a slightly flattened bicone shape.

The way that Diana uses her paddle in shaping is quite different from other techniques that I have seen. Besides the typical rolling the bead on the paddle, she does a lot of circular passes of the paddle over the bead surface. Thus if the bead were being held motionless at the center of a clock, the paddle would be swept around the numbers, tilting the paddle back and forth to smooth the bead surface.

Diana's next step in construction of this bead is to add some colored glass to both ends of the bead. The color that she adds here is the same as the enamel with which she will soon cover the whole surface of the bead. This way as she cleans up any jagged ends of enamel on the bead the glass which shows through will match the rest of the enameled surface. So she wraps a little orange red onto the ends, as in the fourth photo on the left, and then shapes the glass on her paddle to extend the flattened bicone shape, as in the lower left photo.

Diana now builds a clear window that stands tall over the faces. This window makes it easier to locate the portion of the enamel coating, which she will soon apply, that has to be ground away to expose the faces. Diana starts this window by adding a big gather of clear over each of the faces, as in the upper right photo. She then heats the gathers and flattens them with her paddle, causing the clear glass to spread out. She adds additional clear glass as necessary to get it to spread into a roughly rectangular layer, as in the next photo. She shapes this clear layer with the edges of her paddle to get straight edges on the sides of the window, as in the center right photo. She goes back and flattens the front of the window, as in the next photo.

At this point Diana decides that she wants a little more of the base bead below the window than above it. This way it looks a little more like a vessel carrying the family out into the world. So she applies a few stripes of white glass to the bottom and back of the bead, as in the lower right photo, so

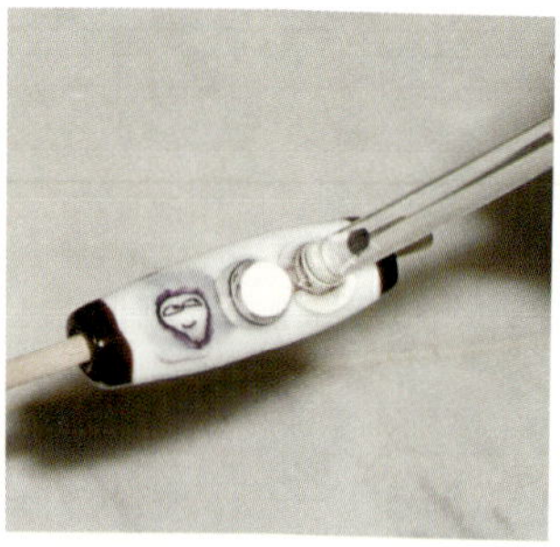

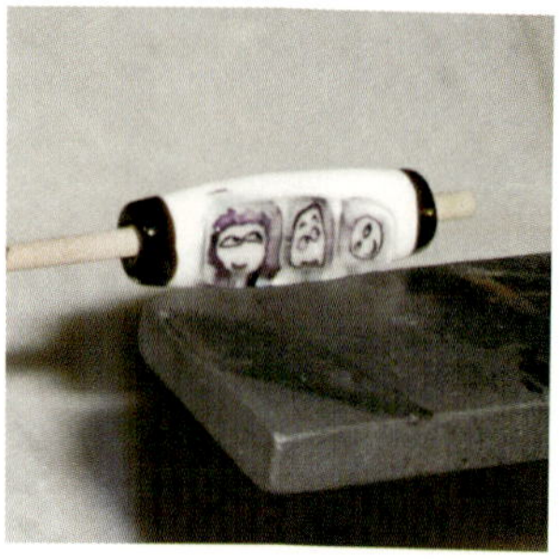

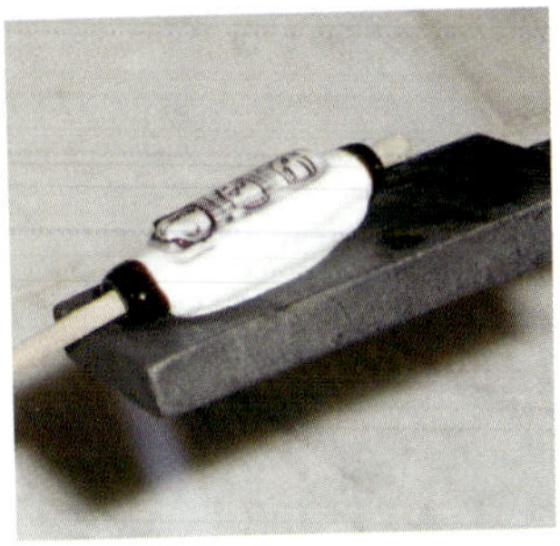

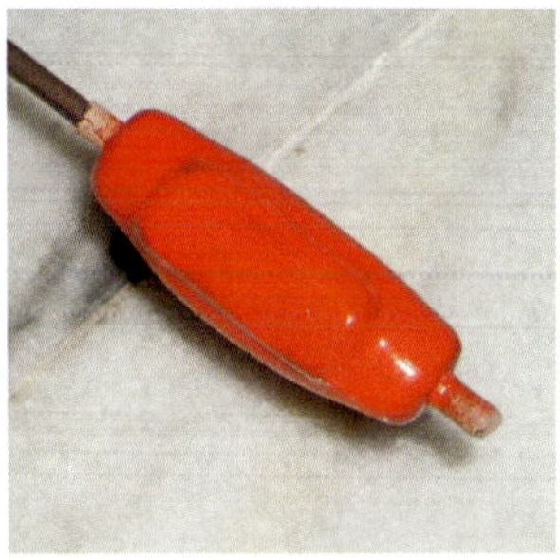

that the bead will hang with the image visible. Diana tests the balance of the bead by holding the mandrel lightly in her hand. She then shapes these areas with her paddle, as in the upper left photo.

The second photo on the left shows the bead after this lower section has been added beneath the rectangular clear window. Diana now coats the entire outer surface of the bead with orange red (#9835) Thompson enamel. She does this through repetitive addition of heat and the powdered enamel that she shakes out of the containers that I discussed earlier. This is what we see her doing in the third and fourth photos on the left. In each case she is shaking the orange red enamel onto the bead after heating it in the flame. Diana is applying the powdered enamel over a sheet of white paper to catch it for recycle.

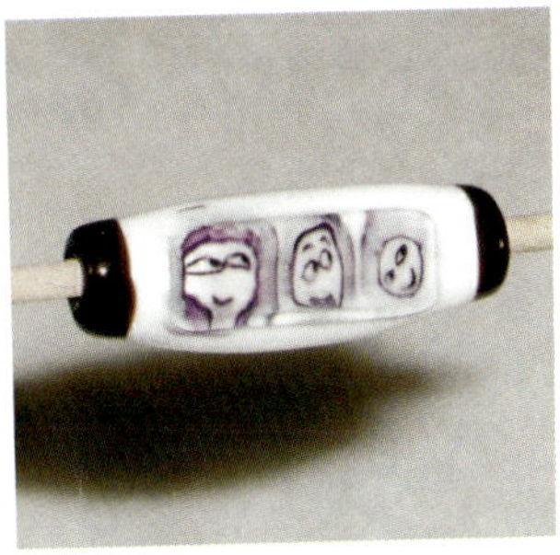

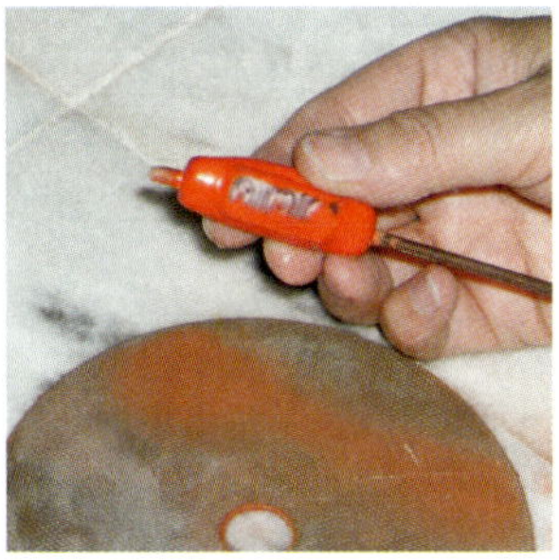

She does one small section at a time, shaking on the enamel and then returning the bead to the flame to melt the enamel into the surface. This also preheats the bead so that the next application of enamel will stick. She has to hold the bead in all sorts of orientations to ensure that the entire surface of the bead gets coated with enamel. Diana then goes back and redefines the shape of the window using the edge of her paddle, as in the lower left photo. This is necessary because all the time in the flame has caused the sharp edges of the window to round slightly. The bead is then put into the kiln to anneal.

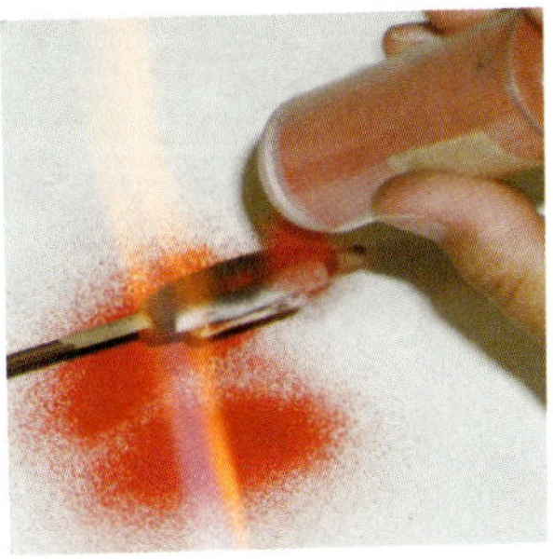

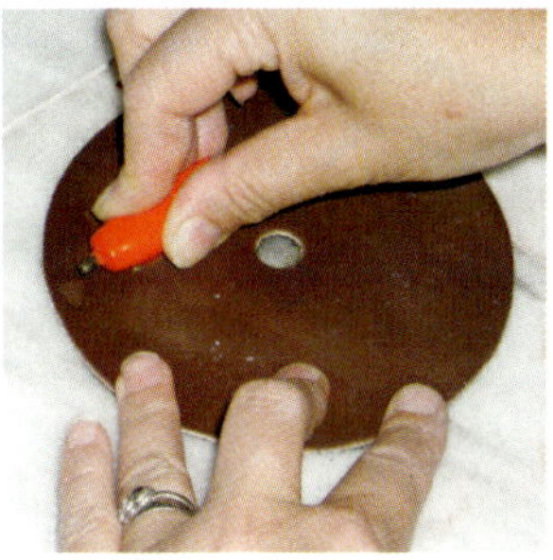

After the bead is removed from the kiln it looks like the upper right photo. The last step is to grind the enamel off the window. Until Diana came up with the idea of the well defined raised window she had a lot of problems determining where to mask and sandblast enamel off of the bead. Here she grinds off the enamel using 6" diameter diamond embedded pads. These can be used on a small lap or by hand as shown. She starts with a coarse grit of 120 until all the enamel is ground off of the window. Then she steps her way to finer grits in stages going to 220, 300, and 600, rinsing the bead well between pads. She uses water as a lubricant as she grinds by hand, checking to make sure the deeper scratches from the previous pad have been removed. She finishes by polishing the window using a slurry of cerium oxide and water on a felt pad, as in the fourth photo on the right.

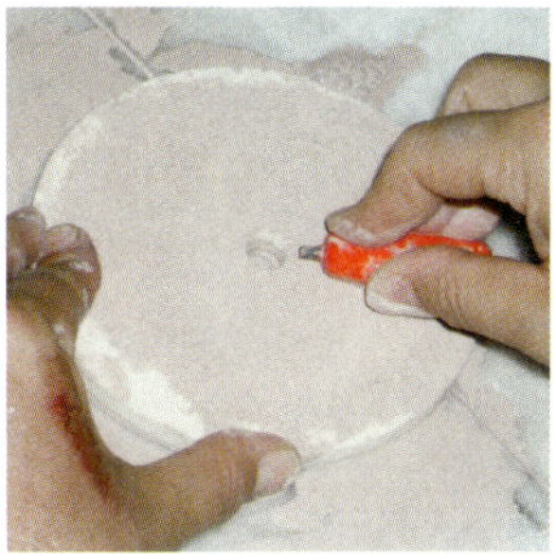

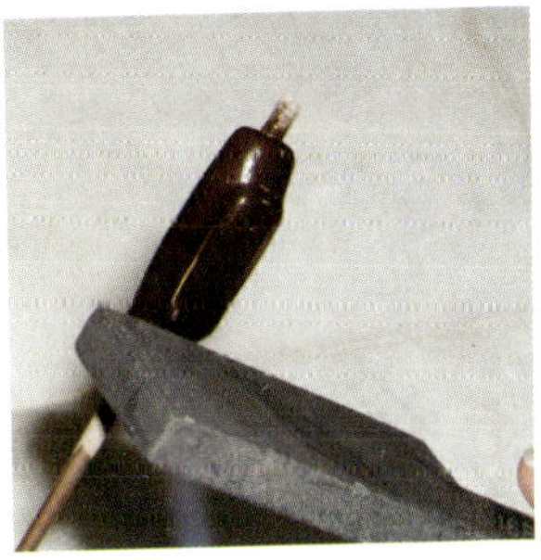

The finished bead is seen in the lower right photo with the faces of the family peaking out of the window. A step that you did not see was Diana grinding the ends flat on a 220 grit stone after removing the bead from the mandrel. This is necessary to remove the short, sharp tube of enamel that builds up on the ends of the bead, as in the upper right photo.

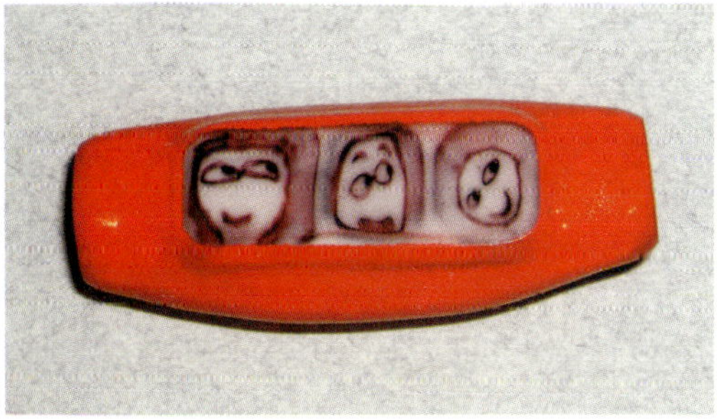

Little Thinker Bead

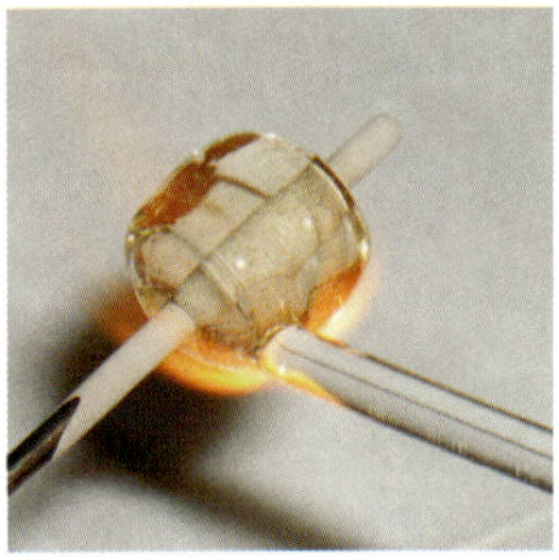

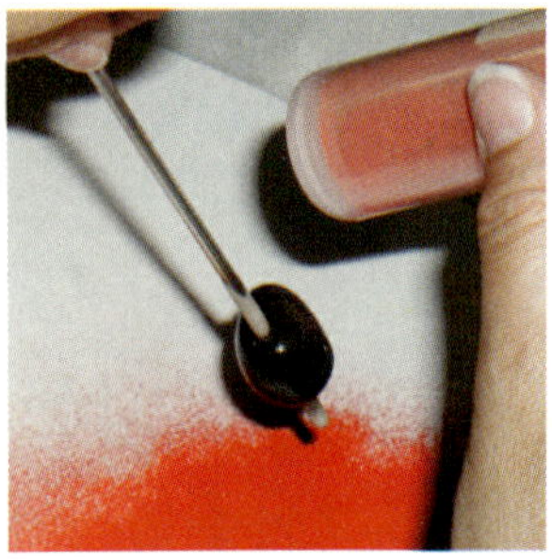

As mentioned, Diana has recently become very interested in the brain and the mystery of how nerves firing can result in such a brilliant thing as consciousness. This bead presents her artistic rendition of the dynamic process of thinking on a molecular level.

Diana starts by building the body of the bead, as in the first four photos to the left. She uses clear glass for the base bead because it is less expensive, it will be colored by the enamel, and also because it is stiffer and will deform less in the heat of the flame. She first winds the bead to length, as in the upper left photo, and then winds on additional clear glass to build up the diameter of the bead, as in the second photo to the left. Notice how with the second layer she continues to work the glass relatively hot as she applies it.

Next Diana rounds up the bead, using the heat of the flame to get the glass hot enough to flow and allowing the surface tension of the glass to round it up. She continues rotating the mandrel to keep the glass centered, as in the center left photo. When the surface is smooth she takes the bead out of the flame, lets it cool slightly while continuing to rotate the mandrel, and then stops rotating it long enough to allow gravity to stretch out the bead to the oblong shape seen in the next photo.

Now Diana coats the outside of the bead with colored enamels. She starts by coating the entire surface with orange red (#9835), as in the lower left photo. She alternates heating the bead with shaking enamel onto it from all possible directions until the bead is uniformly coated. What Diana really wants is a transition from red at the top of the bead to orange at the bottom to represent the action potential wave flowing through the nerve cell, so she applies some bright red enamel (#9840) to the top of the bead, as in the upper right photo. Finally to represent the nerve resting state, she lightly shakes melon orange (#9830) onto the bottom of the bead, as in the next photo. This also adds speckles of melon orange over the orange red in the transition region.

Next Diana covers the surface of bead with random squiggles of black threads, as she is doing in the center right photo. The glass she is using is an intense dark black made by Plowdan and Thompson in Great Britain that is more resistant to bleeding than Effetre intense black. Because the thread heats up so quickly she has to apply the squiggles through the side of the flame.

Diana then adds dot decorations to represent the ion exchange pumps on the outside of the cell that pump sodium ions to the outside and potassium ions into the interior of the nerve cell to build up its resting potential. She starts by adding dots of light sky blue, as in the fourth photo on

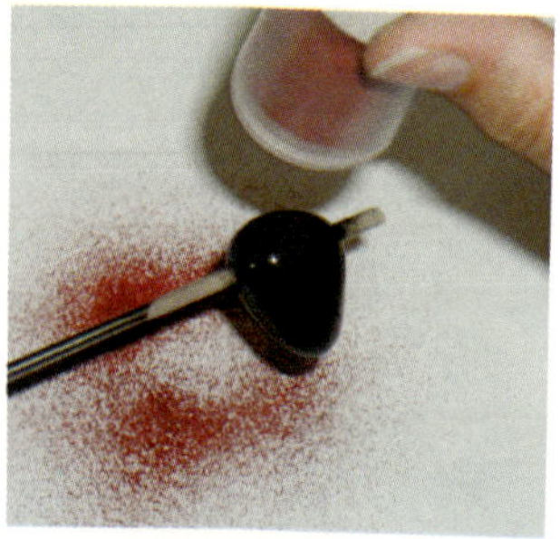

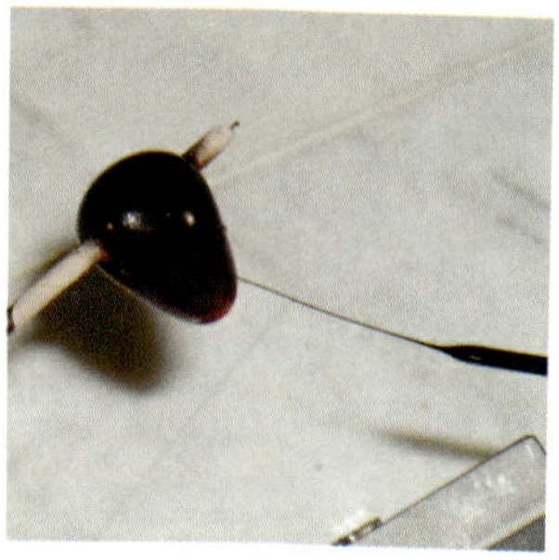

the right. These dots represent the enzyme that transfers the ions across the membrane. She then warms each dot and flattens it on her paddle, as in the lower right photo on the previous page. She applies a slightly smaller purple dot on top of each of the blue dots, as in the upper left photo. She lightly reheats each dot to smooth it out but leaves it rounded and mounded, as in the second photo on the left.

Now Diana adds some stainless steel wire armatures to the bead to represent motion of molecules to and from the cell. To make these armatures she uses small diameter (one sixteenth inch) mandrels that she embeds into preheated spots on the bead, as in the center left photo. For this bead, she is poking the mandrel into some of the dots that she has strategically placed at the bottom and the top of the bead. She pushes longer sections of mandrel into the bead and then cuts them shorter using wire snippers, as in the next photo. This makes handling of the rod easier and burning of her fingers less likely. If the direction of the wire is not quite right, she adjusts it afterward by carefully heating the area and then using her tweezers to manipulate it, as in the lower left photo. If she gets it too hot, the mandrel can burn through.

Next Diana puts in a center bright spot on each purple dot to represent ion exchange. She uses a neat trick that she has for making silver-backed dots. Before starting this bead, Diana cut up part of a sheet of sliver foil into small pieces on a graphite marver and set it aside, as in the upper right photo. She now takes a transparent grass green cane that she has pulled ahead of time, heats the end until it just starts to ball up, and pokes it down onto one of the pieces of silver to pick it up, as in the second photo on the right. Then with the silver stuck to the end of the cane, as in the center right photo, she burns off the excess silver hanging off the cane by heating it very gently just at the edge of her flame while pointing the cane in the direction of the flame.

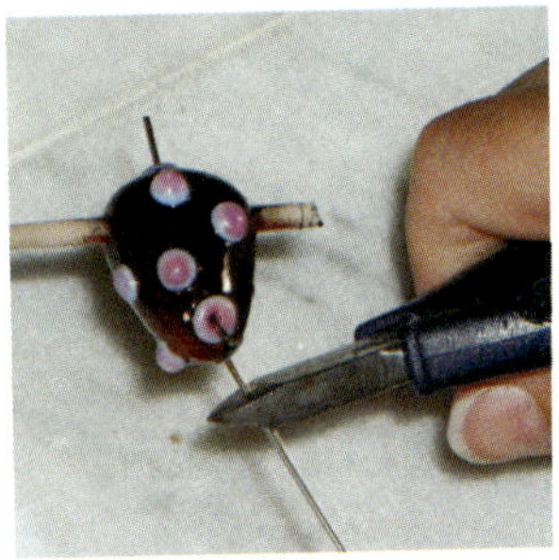

Diana then applies the silver backed dot by heating one of the pink dots and poking the cane into the center of it, as seen in the fourth photo on the right. She flame cuts the excess stringer leaving a cabochon of color with a sharp crease at its edges. If the transparent grass green dot that is left on the bead does not quite have the shape that she wants, Diana can modify it by heating it and flattening it with her paddle, as in the lower right photo. She can also add a dome shape to the dot by reheating it and pressing a nail set onto it, as in the upper left photo on the next page.

Now Diana adds glass balls to each of the embedded wires. She starts with the wire at the head of the bead. This glass ball represents a glutomate neurotransmitter molecule approaching a receptor on the outside of the cell membrane of the nerve. This ball is also the largest of the

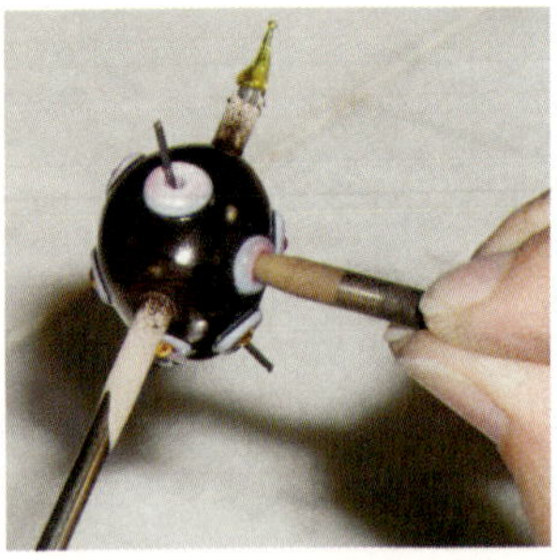

balls that she adds to any of the wires and thus requires adding more glass to it than the rest.

Diana starts the incoming glutomate neurotransmitter by adding a small ball of glass to the end of the wire. She lets the glass set up a little and then winds on additional glass, as in the second photo on the left. She touches a small hot gather of dark transparent aquamarine to the side of the ball and swirls the gather around in a circle around the ball, winding more glass onto it.

Next Diana has to do a balancing act to get the surface tension of the glass to pull it into a sphere. If the glass was on a mandrel, she could rotate the mandrel to hold it in place. She does something similar here by moving her end of the mandrel around in big arcs back and forth while keeping the center of the bead in approximately the same position. The arcs cause small partial rotations of the bead and the wire. She does this dance both hot to form the ball and then as the glass is cooling to retain the ball shape, as in the third and fourth photos on the left. She also tips the wire up or down as necessary depending on whether she wants the ball of glass to slump toward the bead or away from it. She has to keep the large base bead warm through all this too.

Once the ball is shaped and stabilized, Diana adds transparent grass green dots on it, as in the lower left photo. The dots represent the various proteins on the surface of the neurotransmitter. She uses a small cane for this purpose and works in the side of the flame to avoid getting the ball so hot that the glass becomes mobile. After she has applied all the protein dots, she will gently heat each in the side of the flame to adjust their heights equally, as in the upper right photo.

Diana's last step is to add balls on the end of the lower armatures. They represent outgoing neurotransmitters that are being released into the synaptic junctions to excite neighboring neurons. This process is known as exocytosis. These purple balls are made by touching a gather on a purple rod to the end of the wire, as in the second photo on the right. In this case not quite enough glass was transferred this first time and Diana had to add a little additional glass to the ball between this photo and the next. She then goes into the mandrel dance, tipping it back and forth and swinging it in arcs to keep the hot glob of glass balanced on the end of the wire while surface tension and gravity forms it into a ball, as in the fourth photo on the right.

The last photo on the right shows the finished Little Thinker bead. See how the silver backed dots really sparkle and notice the transition of color from red to orange in the enameled surface.

Sandblasting

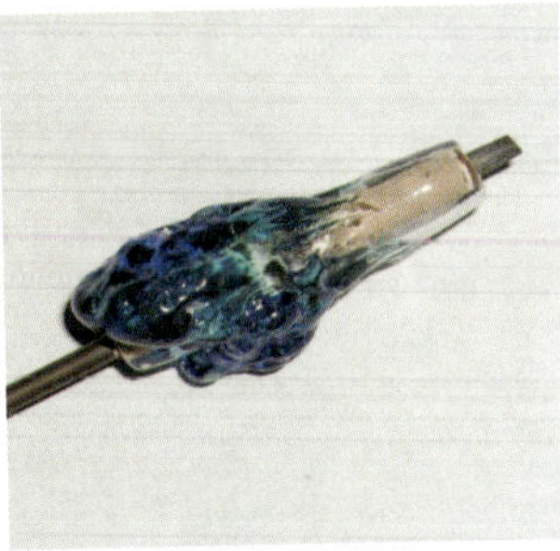

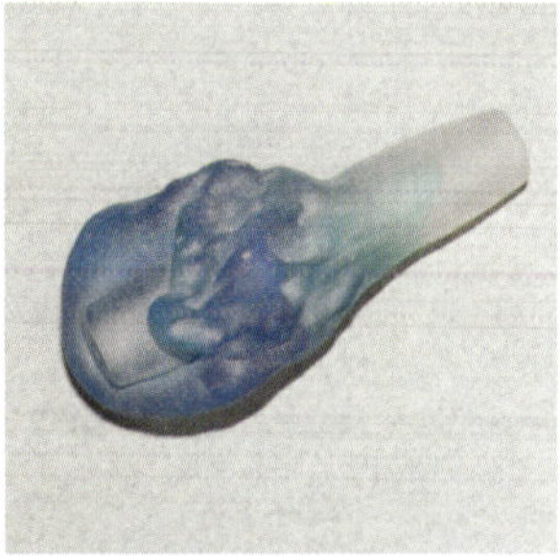

Sandblasting carves glass from the surface of a bead by chipping away small fragments with a fast moving abrasive stream. The preferred abrasive is silica carbide because it is hard and sharp, and when grains break they form sharp edged fragments. We saw in the Wave Bead how blasting changed a smooth surface into a matt finish. Comparing the change in appearance of this bead from the photo of the unblasted bead on the left to the photo of the blasted bead on the right, we see how blasting emphasizes the shape and texture of the bead. This happens for two reasons: first because of etch variation from self-shadowing, and second because etching causes the eye to stop at the surface of the bead and not penetrate into it. Sandblasting also gives us a way to carve colorful decorations into multilayer beads.

The main pieces of equipment that you need are a compressor, a sandblaster, a sandblasting cabinet, and a vacuum system. These components are lined up from right to left in the photo at the top of the next page. The size and cost of the system that you buy will likely depend on the size of the pieces you are going to blast, how often you are going to blast, and your studio space restrictions. Since beads are small you do not need a large system, but if you want to get done fast you may want a robust one.

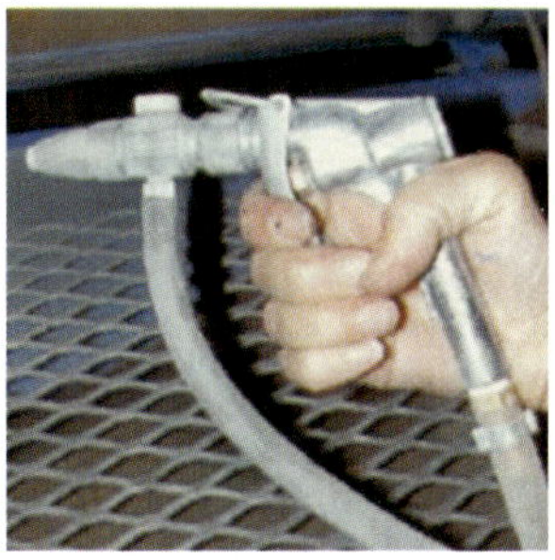

Siphon Gun

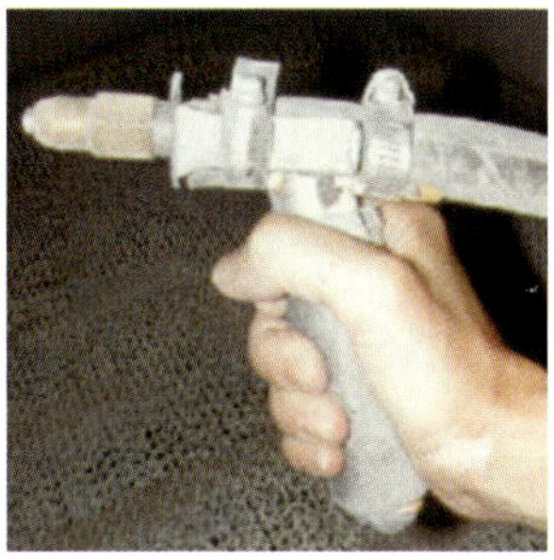

Pressure Pot Gun

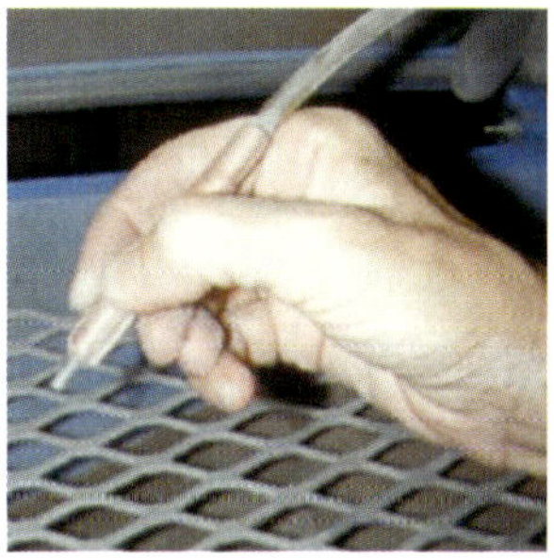

Pressure Pot Pen

Gun Photos by: Bronwen Heilman

There are two basic types of sandblasting systems; siphon and pressure pot. They differ in how much and how hard they deliver the abrasive grit from the sandblasting gun. These factors equate into cutting speed. Siphon systems are the cheapest and slower of the two, but this can also allow more control. Siphon systems work much like a perfume atomizer. Air flowing from the compressor, through the gun, and out the nozzle will pull abrasive up a feed hose from the abrasive hopper, which is usually at the bottom of the cabinet, to the nozzle. It then gets pulled into the air stream and is shot against the bead. The gun configuration for a siphon system can be seen in the photo to the right. The front hose is connected to the hopper and the back hose is connected to the air supply.

In a pressure pot system, the container holding the abrasive is pressurized and as air is fed to the gun through the container it picks up abrasive that builds up speed as it goes through the feed line to the gun and out onto the bead. The abrasive hits the bead much harder than it does from a siphon system. Pressure pot guns, like the one in the second photo to the right only have a single hose attached to them.

Besides guns, which can attack a larger area, there are also sandblasting pens, like the one seen in the third photo to the right. These have smaller nozzles that deliver the grit more locally. By the single hose and its small size attached to the pen, we can see that it is a small pressure pot system operated at lower pressure which will not cut into the glass as quickly as a gun. Pens also do not allow controllability of the abrasive-to-air ratio and suffer from frequent clogging of the orifice.

The figure at the top of the next page shows the large pressure pot system used to make the beads in this booklet. It consists of a 5 horsepower compressor capable of delivering 5 cubic feet of air at 100 pounds per square inch (psi). To its left is the pressure pot with foot switch control. It holds 50 pounds of abrasive fed at a pressure of 60 psi. It is a thick walled vessel and is filled with abrasive through a funnel-like opening at the top and the abrasive air stream comes out the bottom.

To its left is the blasting cabinet. The pressure feed hose comes through a hole in the side of the cabinet to the gun inside. Objects are inserted into the cabinet through hinged window in front, and then you stick your hands into the gloves to operate the

blaster. The cabinet contains all the abrasive and the etched glass, preventing it from getting all over your workspace. Breathing ground glass or silica carbide can cause silicosis, a disease similar to asbestosis, so be sure to let the dust die down before reaching into your cabinet and wear a respirator when using a sandblaster or when cleaning it out.

To the left of the cabinet is a HEPA vacuum to pull the grit out of the cabinet so you can see what you are doing. You will notice how some of the blasting photos in this booklet look hazy. This is because of all the abrasive flying around in the cabinet. Between the vacuum and the blasting cabinet is a small cyclone separator to capture the abrasive sucked out of the cabinet and let the dust go on through. It also saves on wear and tear of the vacuum's motor.

For beads you can probably get by with a small desktop cabinet system. You can find a number of these cabinets with simple siphon systems built into them for about $200. For about $100 more you can find systems that also include a small dust collector to keep your vision clear while blasting. You will still have to purchase a compressor to drive the system but now we are only talking about hundreds rather than thousands of dollars. You might also find places that will blast your beads for you.

Later in this booklet we will discuss the use of resist materials to mask off areas of a bead that we do not want to blast. They also allow developing sharp transitions from unblasted to blasted areas with considerable depth to them. A good resist requires three main properties: first it needs to stick well to the glass during blasting but be easily removable when you are done, second it needs to be strong enough to resist the abrasive action of the sandblaster, and third it should be easy to apply and modify as the job requires.

Typical resist materials that meet these requirements are glues and adhesive backed plastic films. Glues are good for random patterns like squiggles but are hard to make into complex patterns. Good glues to use are milk-based glues like Elmers or hot melt glues. Adhesive backed films, similar to shelf paper, are easier to trim and cut patterns into. Diana uses a vinyl tape for her work that I will discuss in more detail during the description on how to make her Cityscape Bead.

Action Potential Bead

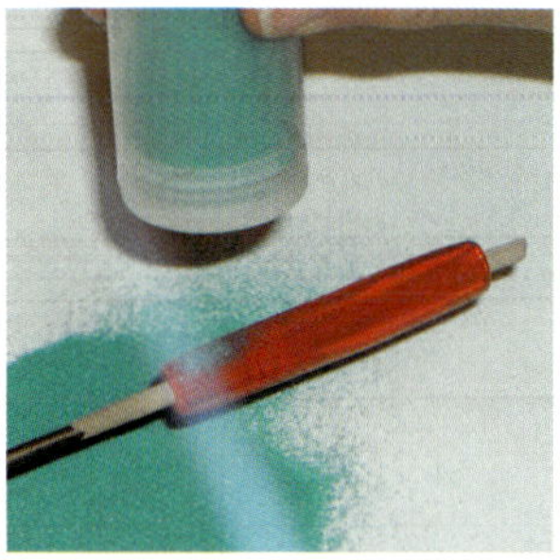

The next bead that Diana will demonstrate for us is one from her Thought Pattern Bead series and incorporates her snakeskin surface finish.

The first thing that Diana does for this bead is to mix a custom color for the thought balls. This is what she is doing in the first three photos on the left. She starts by making a medium sized gather on a transparent grass green rod. She heats the gather until it is glowing and then rolls it in a spoonful of phaseodymium yellow enamel (#9260), as in the first photo on the left. Depending on the depth of color that she wants, she may reheat the gather and roll it additional times in the enamel to pick up more.

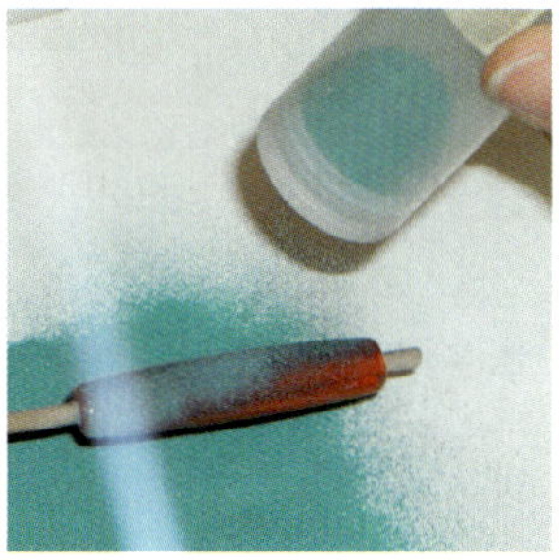

Next to prevent burning off the enamel as she mixes it into the glass, Diana cases the enamel with more transparent grass green. She winds the glass onto the coated gather like she winds a bead on a mandrel, adding successive wraps until all the enamel is covered, as in the second photo on the left. Then she mixes the enamel into the glass by twisting the rods in opposite directions, pushing and pulling on the molten glob as she goes, as in the center left photo. After it's mixed to the point where she can no longer see any striations in the hot glass, she takes it out of the flame for a few seconds to let it cool slightly and slowly stretches it out into the translucent yellow-green cane that we will see on page 19. She has to be careful because too much heat will destroy the color.

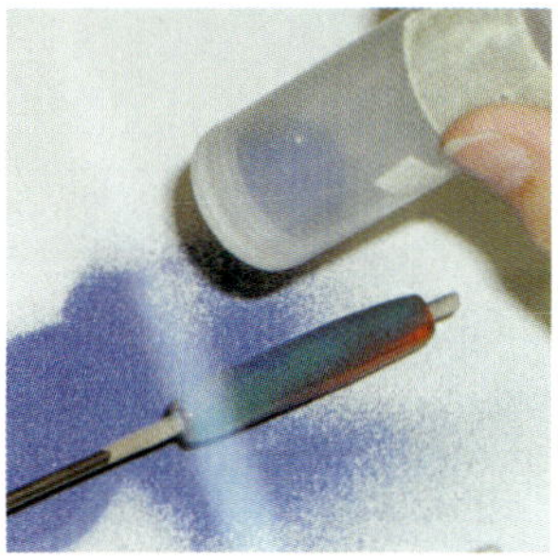

Now Diana begins to construct the base bead using striking transparent yellow, which looks orange when hot. She first winds the glass to length on the mandrel and then adds stripes of glass down the side to build up the thickness and profile of the bead, as in the fourth photo on the left. She applies a thin clear casing, and then smoothes the bead surface by rolling it on her graphite paddle, as in the lower left photo. Clear casing the yellow prevents it from reacting with the blue enamel, which would give a sludgy color.

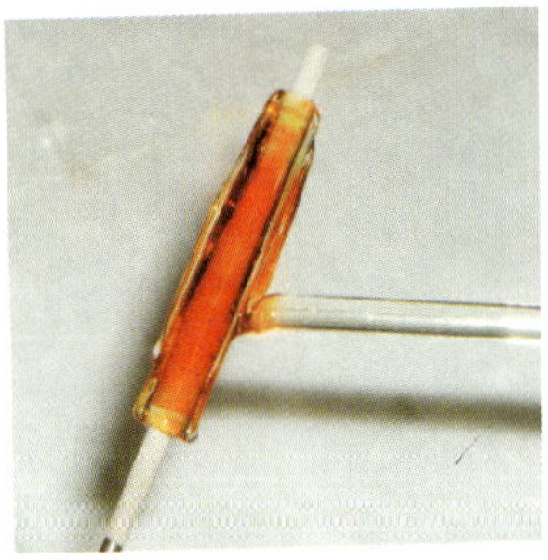
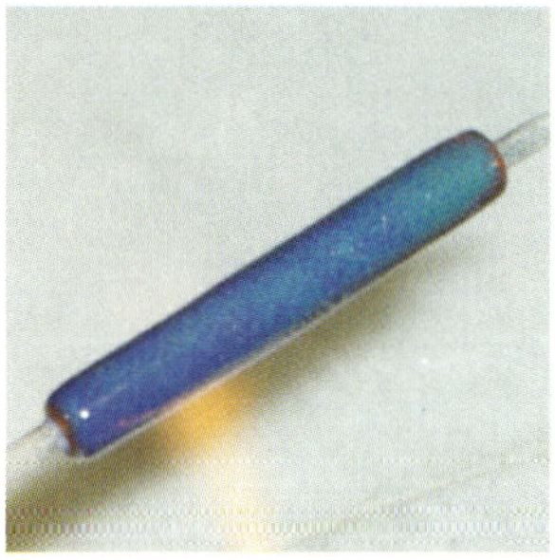

Diana wants variation in color across this bead so she adds two layers of colored enamel that don't necessarily have to go all the way around the bead. She starts with aquamarine enamel (#9550), shaking it onto the hot surface of the bead, as in the two photos to the upper right. She applies the aqua about three quarters of the way around the bead circumference by repeated heating and application cycles. She then adds a smaller coating of Oxford blue enamel (#9650) using the same process, as in the center right photo, and finishes with a little brilliant blue (#9660). The blue side of the coated bead can be seen in the fourth photo on the right.

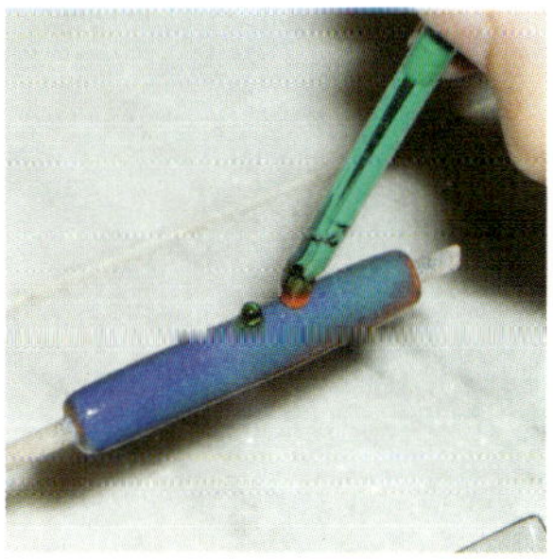

Next Diana apples a regular series of transparent teal dots that will form the snakeskin color variation on the surface of

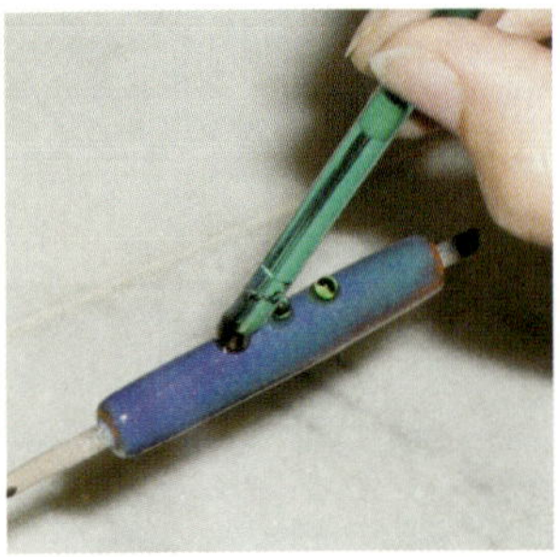
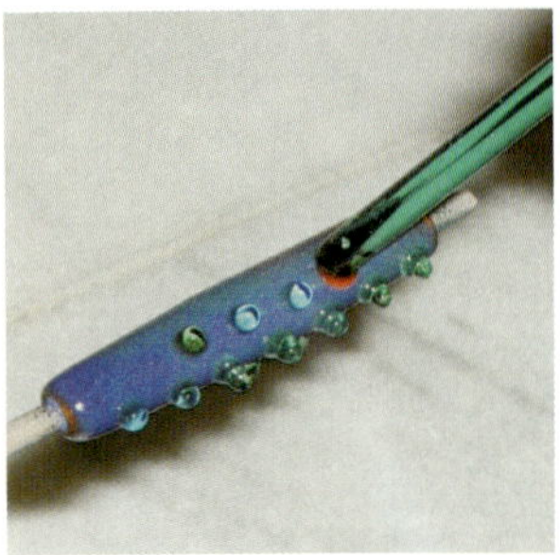
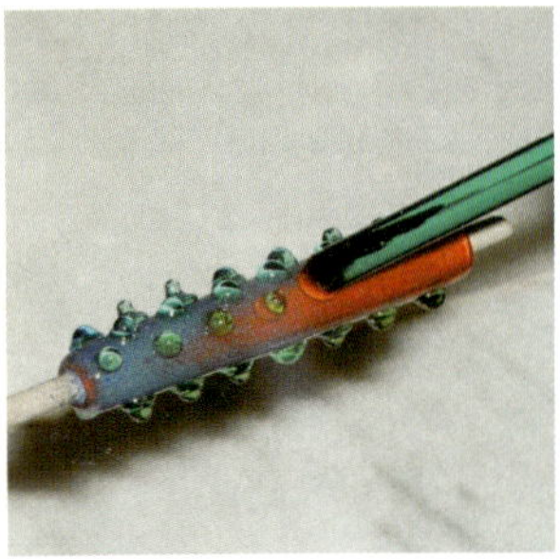

the bead. She centers her dot pattern on the bead by starting application with a single dot at the center of one side of the bead and then works outward by adding equally spaced dots to either side of this dot moving out to the ends of the bead, as in the first photo to the left.

After she finishes the first row of dots, Diana rotates the bead about one-eighth of a turn and adds the next row of dots. The dots in this row are applied axially between the dots of the first row, as in the second photo on the left. She tries to add approximately the same amount of glass to each dot and can add additional glass if a dot appears too small, but messing about too much can disturb the soft enamel. The center left photo shows two dots in the upper left where she added extra glass. This photo also shows her applying dots to the uncoated yellow section of the bead. In all, she adds eight rows of dots to the beads. At this point the bead looks like the fourth photo on the left.

Now comes the point where Diana has to work the dots into the bead surface to form the little pools of transparent green glass. This is where many artists go wrong and Diana says that she is always getting questions on how she achieves this effect. The typical thinking is to just heat things up and sink the dots into the surface of the bead. But if you try this, you will find that the highly fluxed and mobile enamel will flow over the top of the dot as it sinks into the bead surface, covering it up.

Instead Diana works the bead cooler without a lot of flow and patiently forces each dot into the surface of the bead as is demonstrated on this page. Basically she heats one row of dots at a time and pushes down on it with her paddle. She pushes either from above as in the lower left photo or from below as in the upper right photo. She holds the paddle so that she can sight through the gap between it and the bead to gage how much she is compressing the row each step of the way. If need be, she will rock the paddle slightly from end to end to uniformly hit each dot. She goes a little bit at a time at avoid smashing the dots too much, making them larger and not getting them deep enough into the surface. In the lower left photo Diana is paddling the dots for the first time and at this point is just flattening them into short cylinders of about half their original height. This is the stage that she has attained in the upper right photo.

From this point on the process is like working a row of murrine into the bead surface. She has to get the bead hot enough to push the dot into it but the dot is also getting hot enough that if she were to immediately push down on it, the dot would mash and spread out. So what Diana has to do is heat up the row, then lightly bring the paddle into contact with the dots and hold it there for a moment or two before

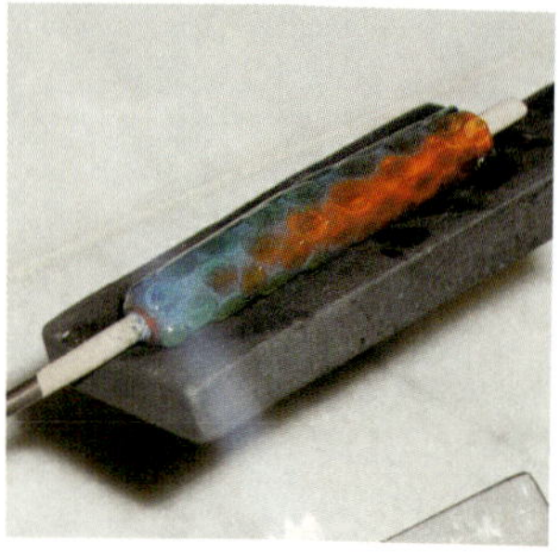
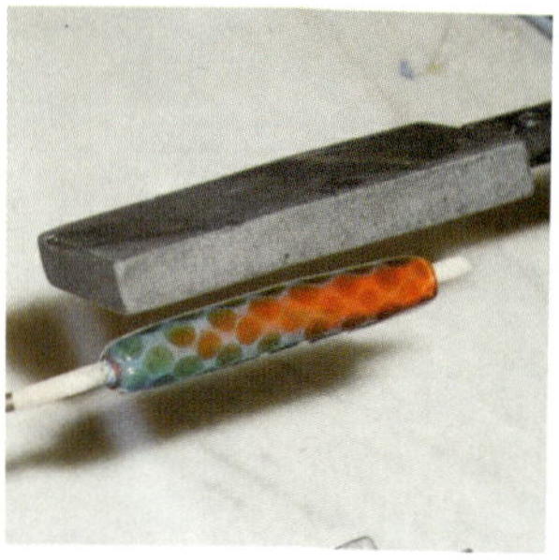
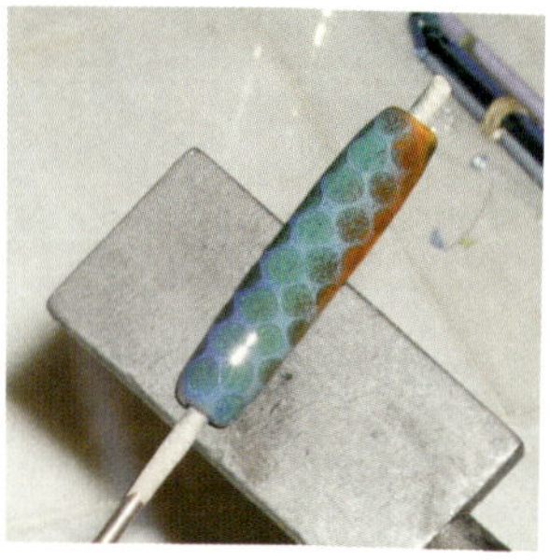
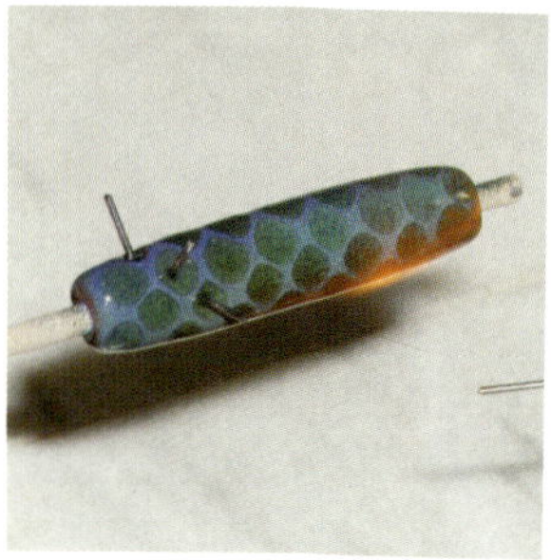

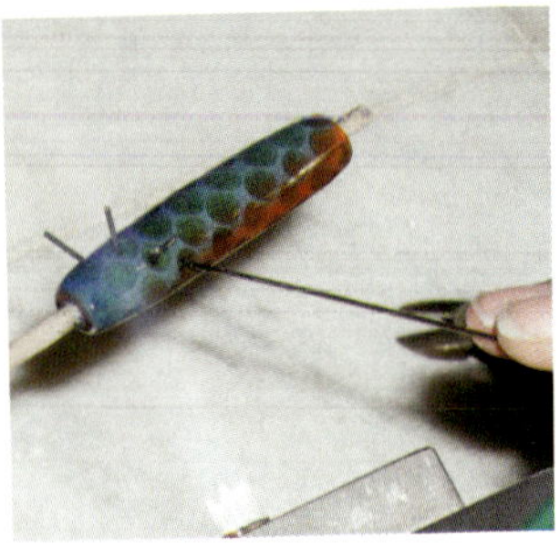
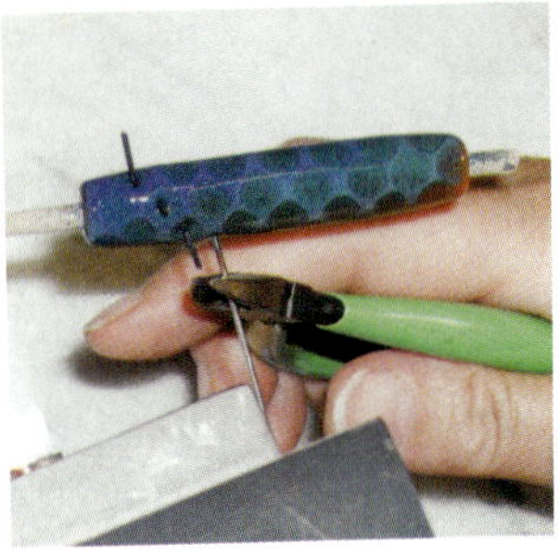
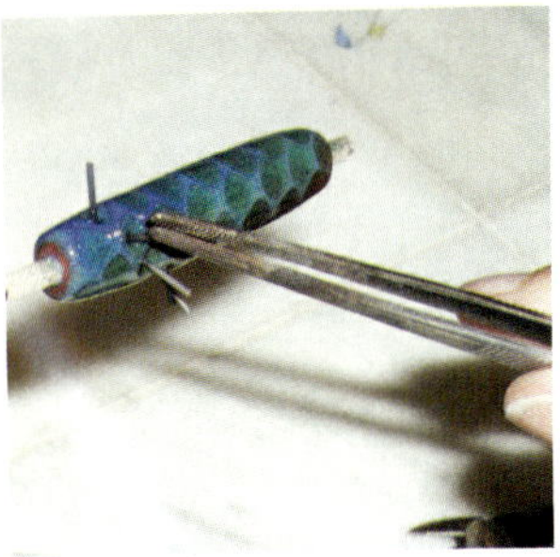

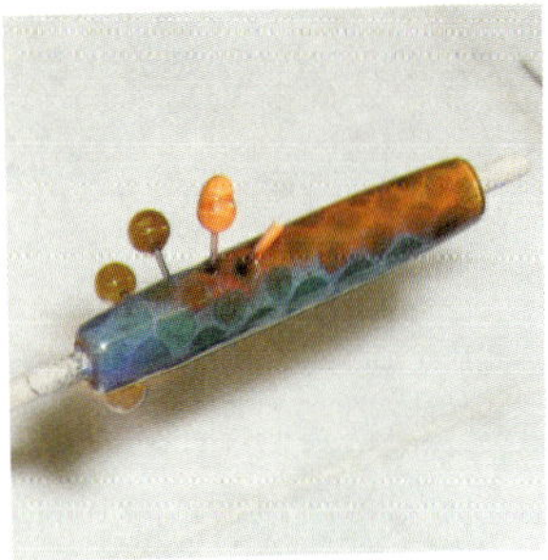

beginning to push. This allows the glass in the dots to chill and harden while the glass in the bead is still relatively soft. When she finally applies pressure, the hard dots are pushed into the softer bead, as in the second and third photos on the right of the previous page. She finally ends with smoothing the surface by heating and rolling it on her paddle, as in the fourth photo on the right of the previous page.

Next Diana embeds five short sections of mandrel wire into the bead. Again the mandrels that she uses for this are the thin one sixteenth of an inch diameter stainless steel. Here she is installing them in the form of an arc of wires coming radially out from the surface of the bead. The beginning of this arc with the first three wire segments in place can be seen be seen in the last photo on the previous page. The first three photos on this page review the wire insertion process where she first heats a spot on the bead, she next pushes the end of a mandrel into the soft spot and then cuts the embedded mandrel to length using wire snips. After all five pieces are embedded; she tweaks them with her tweezers to get them positioned into a smooth spiral.

Now Diana adds balls at the end of each wire using the translucent green color that she mixed earlier. This is shown in the next three photos. She first makes a small gather on the end of the cane and applies it to the wire. Then using the balancing act discussed before, she keeps the hot glob of glass balanced on the end of the wire while gravity and surface tension pulls it into a ball. After all the balls are in place and stabilized, Diana will go back and tweak the wires again, as in the second photo on the right, to get them back into position because they sometimes move a little during ball installation.

The bead is then transferred to the kiln for annealing. When it comes out of the annealer it has a shiny finish as in the center right photo. The dot pools are not very visible here and the bead looks a little flat at this point.

What Diana really wants is a matt finish on the bead. So she transfers it to the sandblaster and lightly blasts the entire surface of the bead, as in the fourth photo on the right. During this process she blasts a little more from the yellow side of the bead than the blue side. This extra blasting will result in a variation to the depth of etch, enhancing the yellow to green to blue transition that is so very visible on the finished bead, as in the last photo on the right. Notice how much more visible the dot pools or snakeskin effect is after blasting. Part of the reason for this is that the enamel is captured under the dot but is partially blasted off the surface surrounding the dots, thus increasing the color contrast.

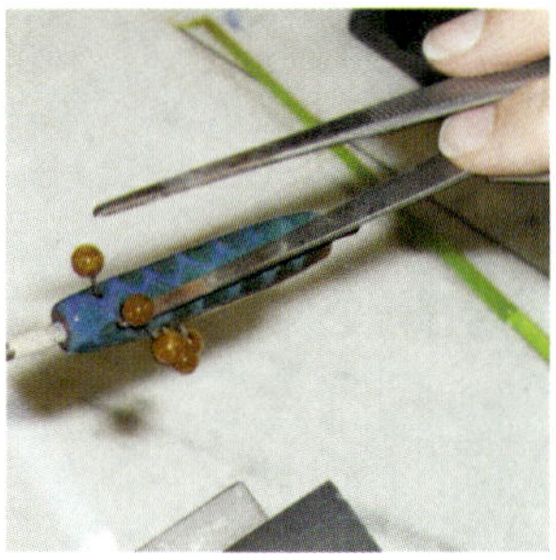

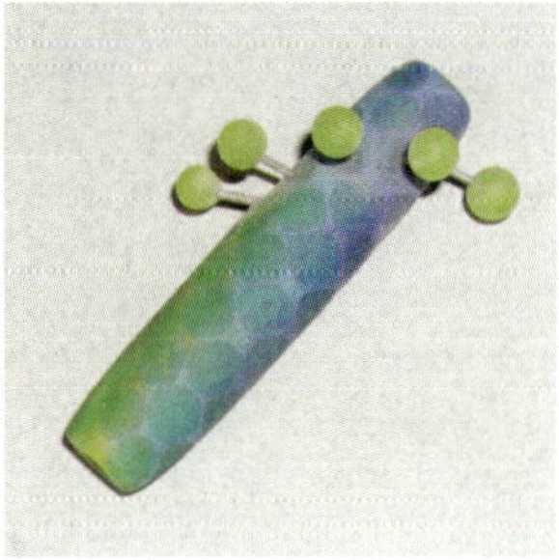

Thought River Bead

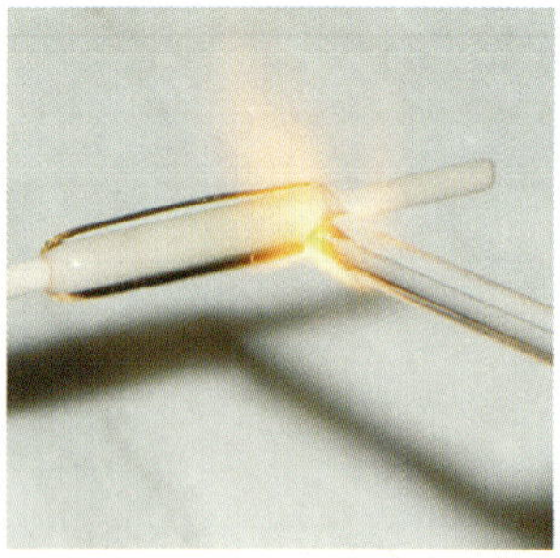

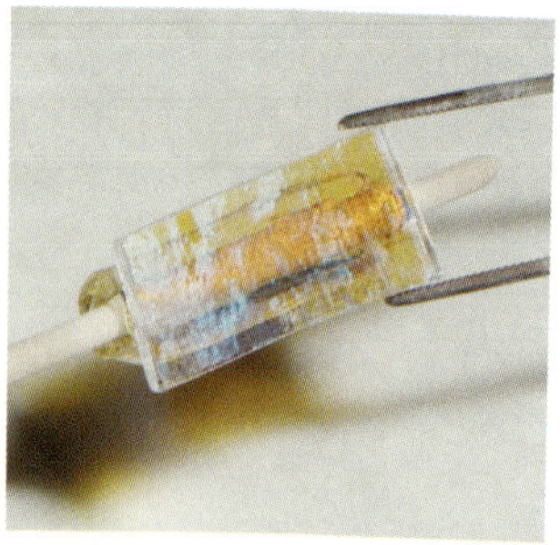

Diana's inspiration for this bead came from the movie, *The Matrix*. It has an ordinary external view of reality, but if you look through the cracks you can see a different version of reality hidden beneath the ordinary level of perception. In this case that translates to a bead with an external enamel veneer with cracks machined into it to reveal a hidden dichroic core.

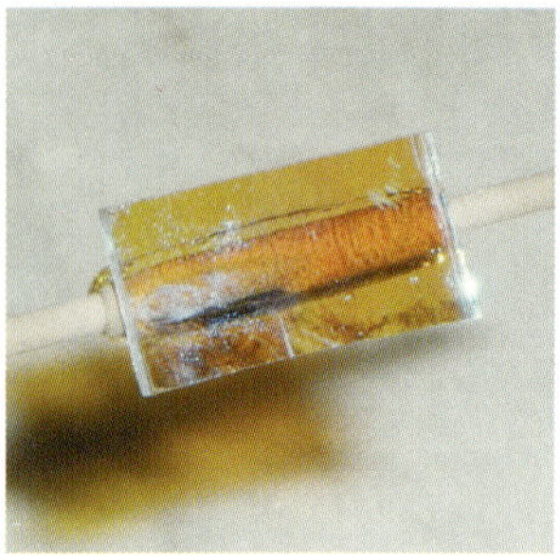

Diana starts this bead with a smooth cylindrical core that she winds on hot, as in the upper left photo. She winds this bead to a length that matches some precut rectangles of dichroic glass. She next applies one of the rectangles of dichroic sheet with the dichroic surface down, as in the second photo on the left. This glass was warmed just enough to stick to the clear core. She then moves it all the way out in the flame, as in the center left photo, to heat it slowly so that the dichroic will not thermal shock.

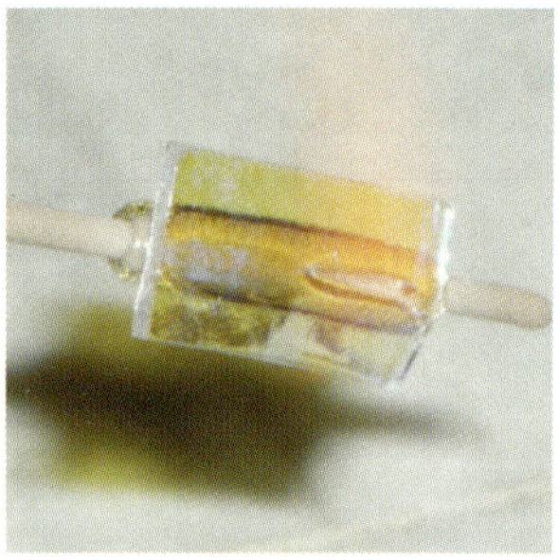

As the glass heats up she moves it closer in the flame and presses on the edges of the rectangle with her tweezers, as seen on the right, to get the glass to bend and conform to the base bead. The last two photos on the left show two steps along the way in this process. First where the dichroic piece has started to bend and conform to the clear core and second where it has completely conformed to the core but has a gap because the dichroic rectangle was narrower than the circumference of the core.

Diana then repeats this process with a second rectangular sheet of dichroic glass that she applies over the gap seen in the lower left photo. The first three photos on the right side of the page show her adding and shaping this dichroic piece with her tweezers, which she keeps cool so they will not stick to the glass. One thing this series illustrates is how she tries to roll down the edges and attach the clear base glass of the dichroic to the bead. She does not want to leave any of the dichroic coating exposed to the flame as that could allow it to fry.

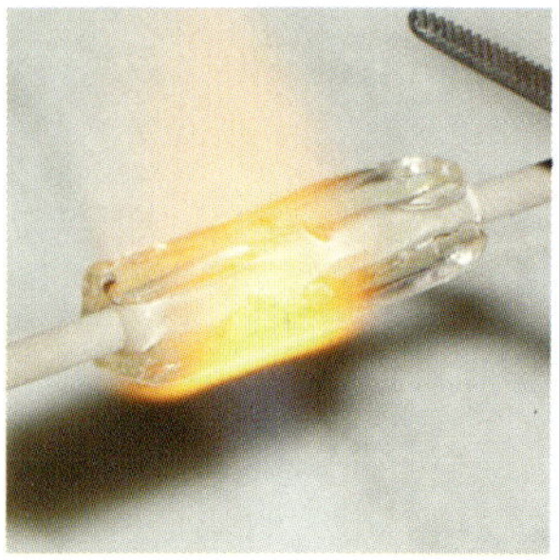

In the last two photos on the right Diana is finishing the base bead before coating it with enamel. In the first of these she is adding clear glass to fill the gap left by the second piece of dichroic. She also adds clear to the ends of the bead to perfect them. She smoothes the surface of the bead by rolling it on her paddle, as in the lower right photo. She flattens it slightly between her paddle and the minimarver mounted on her torch to give it a lozenge shape, after which she lightly heats the bead and works it with her circular paddle passes to refine its shape and remove the chill marks seen in the upper left photo on the next page.

Now Diana applies the enamel veneer which forms the external view of reality for this bead. She spot sifts both brilliant blue and aquamarine enamel, as in the second

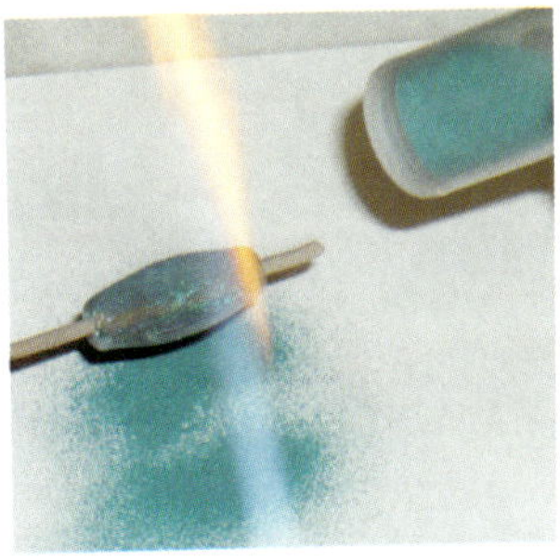

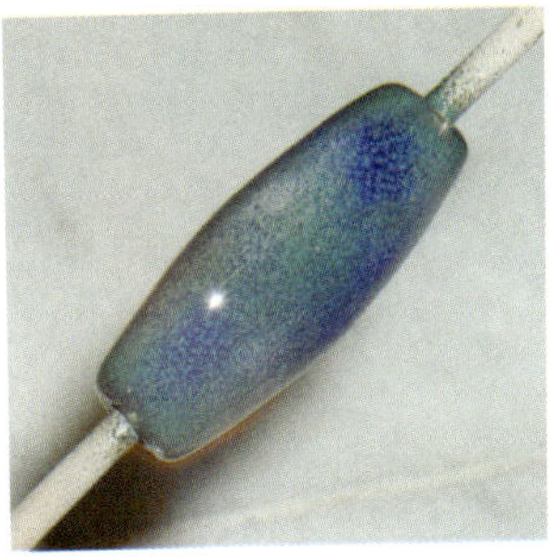

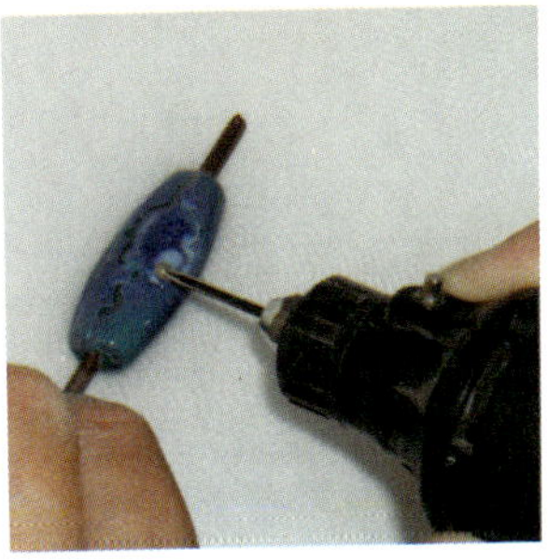

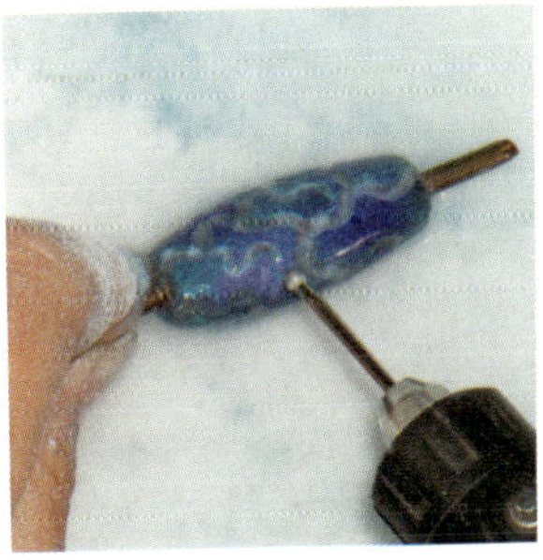

photo on the left. The color variations makes the surface look like satellite photos of earth. After coating, the bead is put into the kiln and well annealed to resist all the cutting she will do on it. The center left photo shows the enamel coated bead after it has come out of the kiln. The bead is kept on the mandrel for ease of handling.

The next step has Diana cutting cracks into the beads enameled surface. Through these gaps in the external view of reality, rivers of flowing thought, are exposed. She cuts these cracks in the enamel coating using a diamond bit mounted in a rotary hand tool. The head of the diamond bit is a ball about an eighth of an inch in diameter. Since the bead has to be worked wet to lubricate the diamond bit and avoid spraying glass dust into the air, it is suggested that a flexshaft extension be used on the tool to avoid electrical shock hazards. The bit is lubricated by frequently dipping it and the bead into water. As can be seen in the lower left photo, Diana is working directly over a dish of water. She cuts squiggling cracks into the surface until it is completely covered with them.

Freshly ground cracks have a frosty appearance and obscure viewing of the internal dichroic core. To rectify this situation the ground surfaces need to be fire polished. To do this Diana sticks the bead still on the mandrel into the cold kiln and brings it up to 10° above the annealing temperature. Then she reaches in and grabs the hot mandrel with a damp folded paper towel so that she can handle it, as in the upper right photo. You could also reach in with some hemostats to grab the mandrel up near the bead and then dip the opposite end of the mandrel in water to cool it enough to handle. Diana quickly introduces the bead back into the flame. Once she gets the bead into the flame she heats it up to the point where the bead is lightly glowing before returning it to the kiln for annealing. When it comes out of the kiln the cracks will be shiny as in the second photo on the right.

Unfortunately, after fire polishing the exterior of the bead will also be bright and shiny. Since Diana wants this version of reality to be a little drab, she decides to acid etch the bead exterior to take the shine off it. We will discuss acid etching in more depth later, but the first step in the process is protecting the areas that are not supposed to be etched. Diana applies nail polish for resist, as in the center right photo. After it is dried she puts the bead in etching solution for a number of minutes to get a matt surface. Then she dips the bead into a solution of baking soda and water to neutralize the acid and finally rinses it in clear water.

The final bead after drying and removal of the nail polish can be seen in the lower right photo.

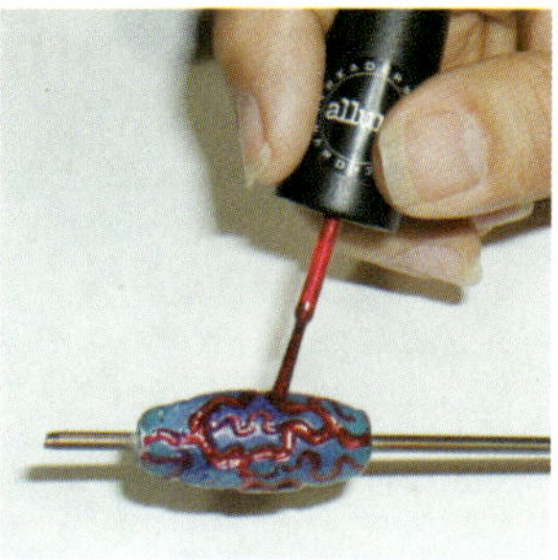

Ancient Blasted Bead

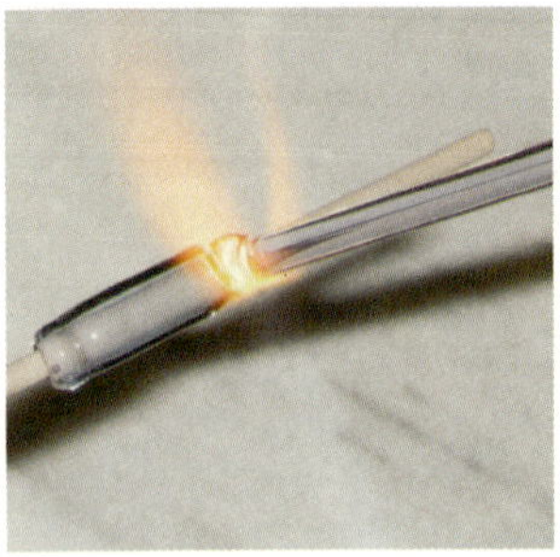

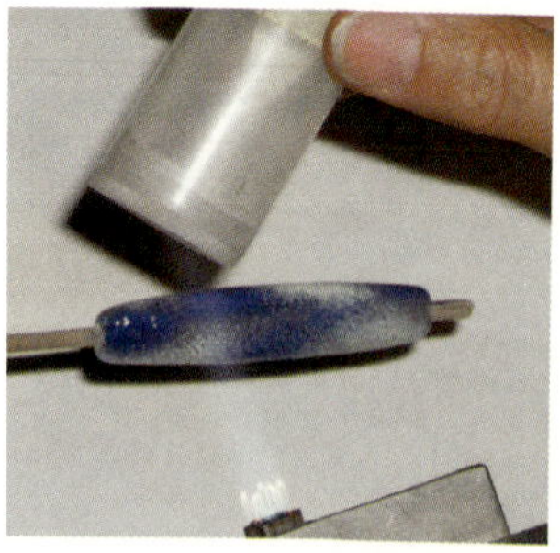

Earlier in her career Diana used to make a lot of beads with an ancient look to them. Because I really liked those beads and it involves some new techniques for you to learn, I convinced her to demonstrate a few of them. This first one is a semi-monochromatic bead with areas sandblasted away to look as if it has been etched away by water for years. This demonstration will also introduce the use of masking media when sandblasting isolated areas on a bead.

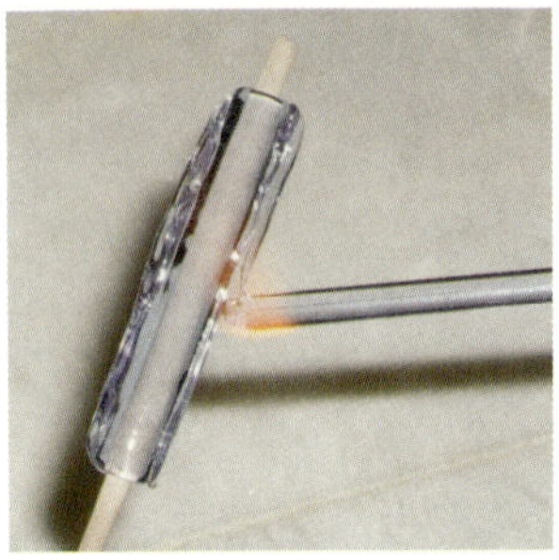

Diana starts as usual by making the base bead, in this case from a light transparent blue. She first winds the bead to length, as in the upper left photo. Then she builds up its cross section by painting on additional glass down the length of the bead, as in the second photo. After smoothing this bead becomes a long barrel, as in the center left photo.

Next Diana lightly and spottily coats the bead surface with enamel. This is supposed to give it a randomly aged look. She first shakes on some brilliant blue enamel (#9660) deliberately leaving some sections of the bead uncovered, as in the fourth photo to the left. When done this first portion of the coating will look like the lower left photo. See how considerable areas of the transparent glass still show through.

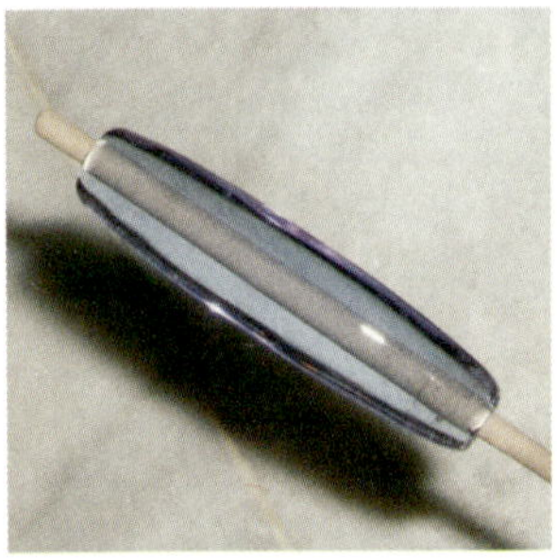

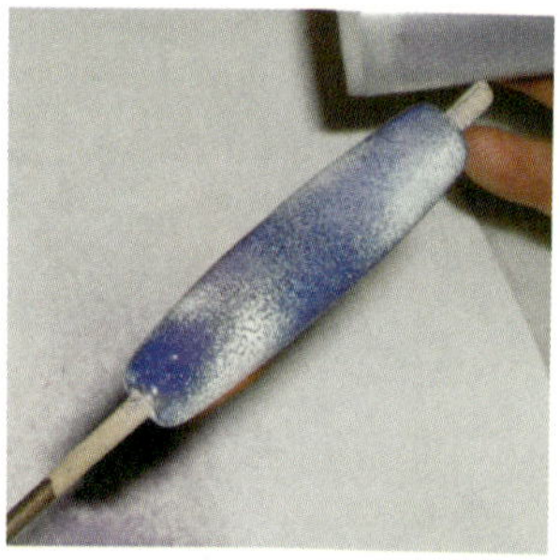

Now Diana applies some small splotches of white by shaking white enamel (#9010) onto some of the clear areas of the bead, as in the upper right photo. After this step the bead looks like the second photo on the right. Finally Diana applies a light dusting of new purple (#9740) over the surface of the bead, as in the center right photo. Notice how even at this point there are still areas of the bead without any enamel on them.

Diana next creates a corroded texture on the surface of the bead. She does this by rolling the bead in baking soda, as in the fourth photo on the right. The cast iron kitchen scoop that she uses here is good because its open end allows easy access to a long trough of soda. When the bead is returned to the flame, as in the lower right photo, the baking soda will cause the glass to boil, giving the surface of the bead a rough matt and pitted texture something like a sand coating. The degree of pitting can be increased by using a more oxidizing flame and by repeating the process. The upper left photo on the next page shows what this bead looked like after a single dip in the baking soda and use of a neutral flame. You also have to get these bicarbonate beads into the annealer right away because the rough surface makes them more susceptible to cracking.

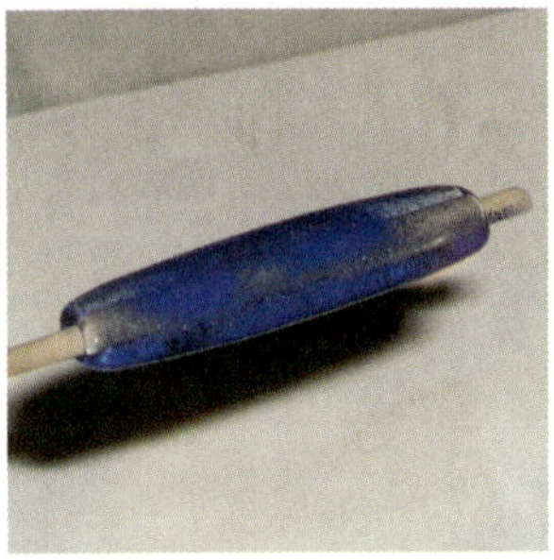

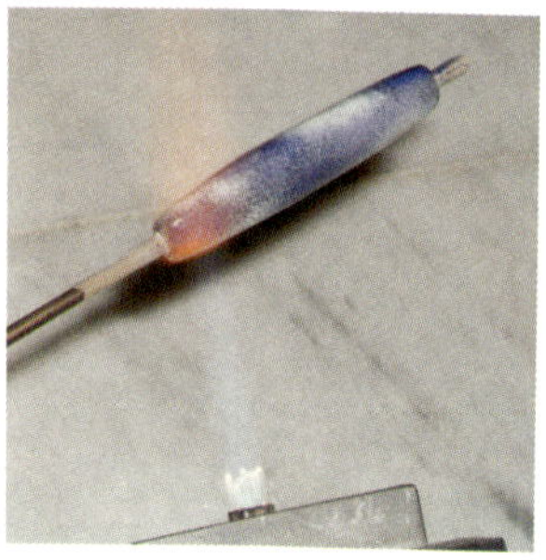

The last step in construction of this bead is to sandblast

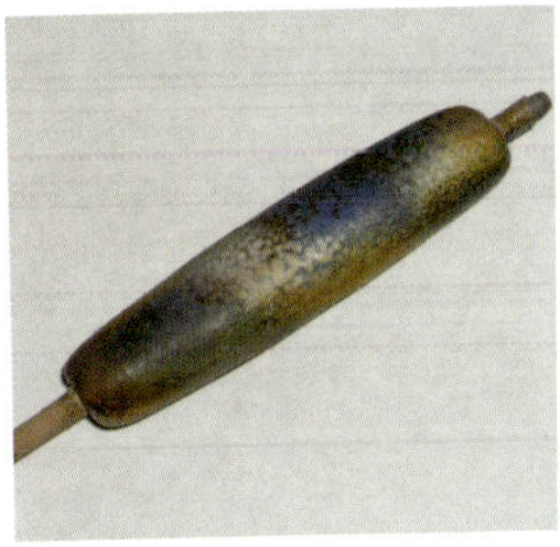
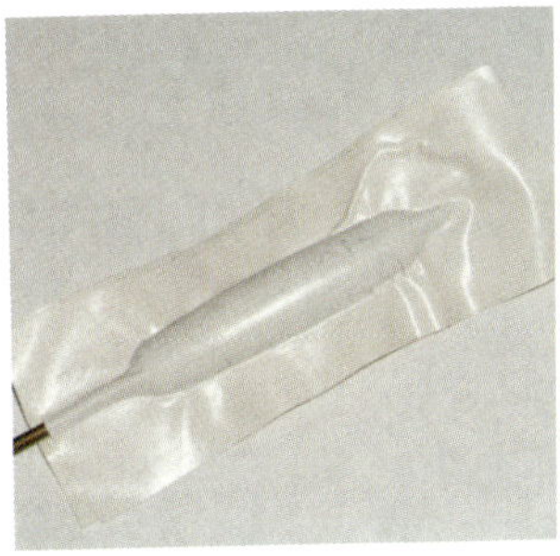
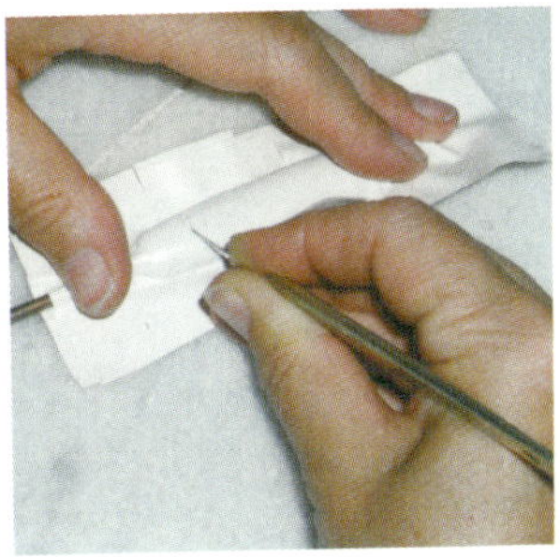
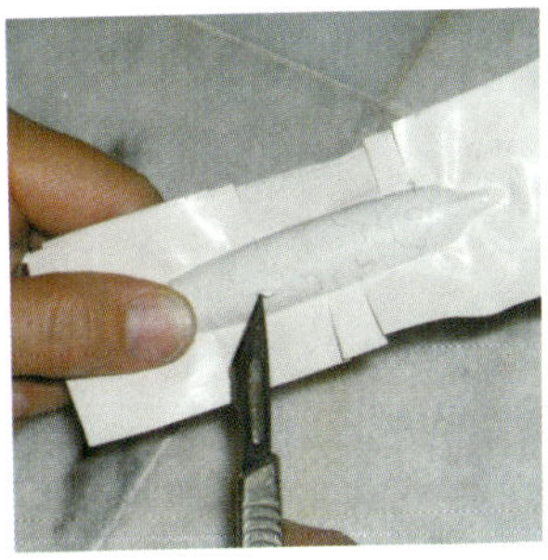
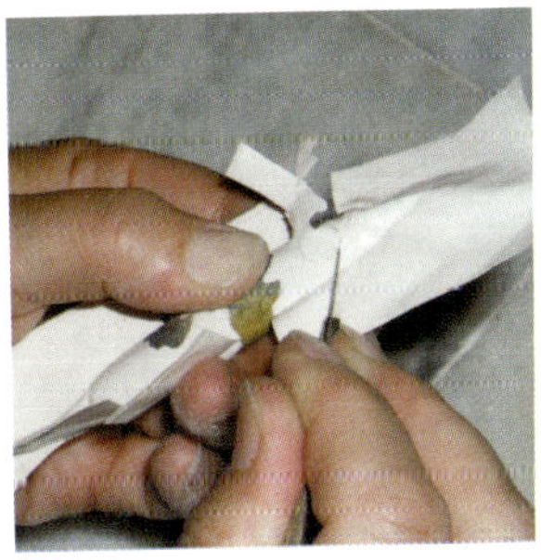

localized areas. She could try to move the bead closer to the nozzle and tap on the sandblaster foot control to do this, but the result would still be a larger blasted area than she really wants and the transition from the blasted to the unblasted areas would not be sharp. To limit the area that gets blasted and guarantee sharp transitions, Diana uses masking material that leaves exposed only those areas of the bead that she wants blasted. The second photo on the left shows the bead after she has covered the whole surface with resist. The material that she is using is a vinyl masking tape about two inches wide, which we will discuss in greater detail for the Cityscape Bead. She has run it down one side of the bead, folded it and run it down the other side of the bead. She has to burnish and stretch the tape to insure that it conforms to and is well bonded to the surface of the bead.

Next Diana defines the areas of the bead that she is going to blast by sketching them onto the sandblasting resist with a soft lead pencil. Where it crosses the tape plane, she extends the contact point out to the edge of the tape and over to the other side. After she has her blasting plan laid out, Diana cuts through the masking with a sharp scalpel. She cuts perpendicular to the bead surface following the lines laid out on the masking, as in the center left photo. Notice how she has to cut all the way out to the edge of the tape. After a little while, the tip of the scalpel can get dull. She sharpens it as necessary on a small sharpening stone.

After Diana has cut through the resist along the length of the blasting plan, she peels off the tape from the areas that she wants to blast, as in the last two photos on the left. She may occasionally find small sections where the scalpel did not completely cut through the tape and will have to recut that section. After she has removed all the tape from the areas where she wants to blast, the bead looks as in the upper right photo. She checks thoroughly to make sure that she has also removed all the glue, especially in the tight corners.

Now Diana is ready to blast and she moves the bead into the sandblaster, as in the second photo on the right, and blasts the exposed areas of the bead. The center right photo shows the bead after blasting. She has blasted through the enamel layer and into the transparent glass below, but because the surface is matt it is only translucent. The next photo shows Diana removing the masking to expose the finished bead, which is shown in the lower right photo. Here you can see how sharply defined the transitions from blasted to unblasted areas are and how well the blasted surface mimics glass having been eaton away by water with time.

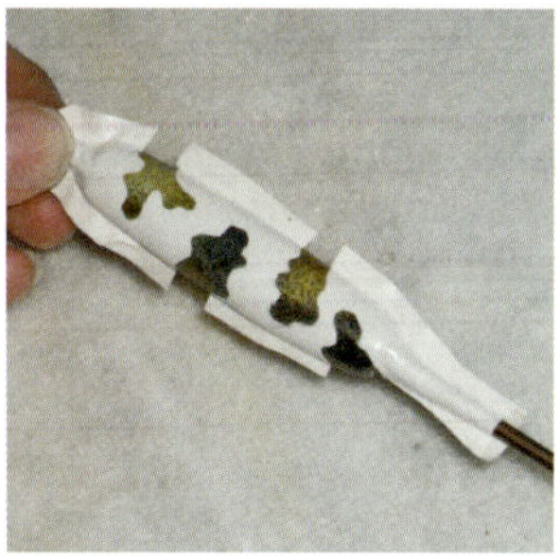

Ancient Eye Bead

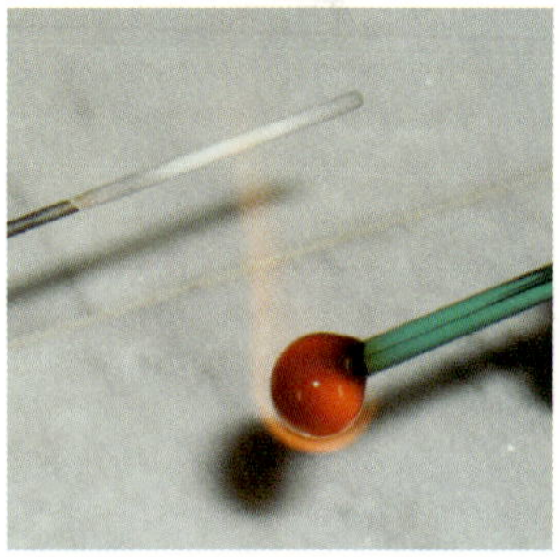

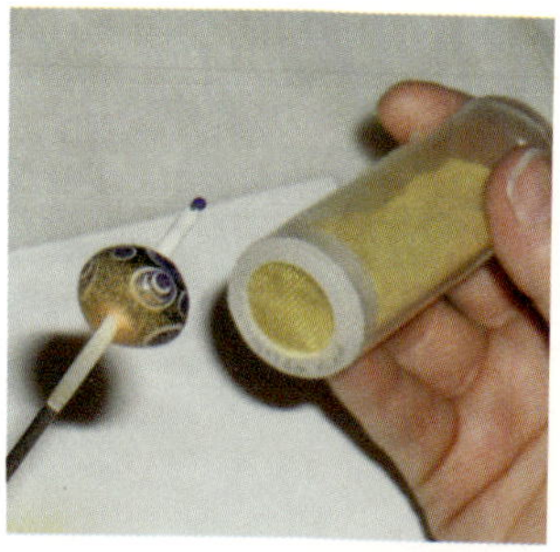

The second design inspired by ancient beads that Diana is going to demonstrate is an eye bead. This is an ancient Chinese style, and she got the idea for this bead while looking through the "The History of Beads" by Lois Sherr Dubin. This book has served as the inspiration for a number of her "ancient reproductions."

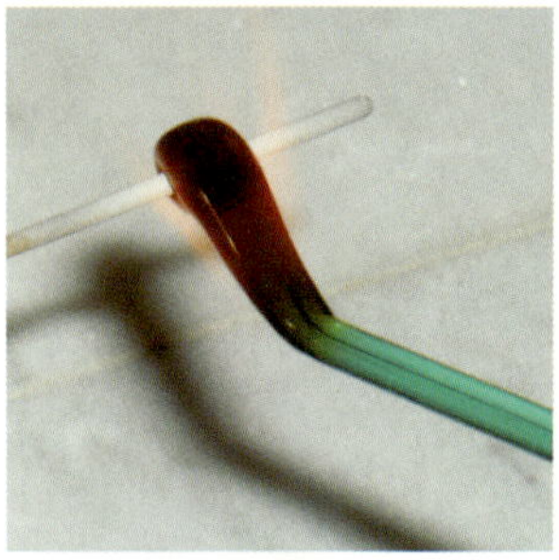

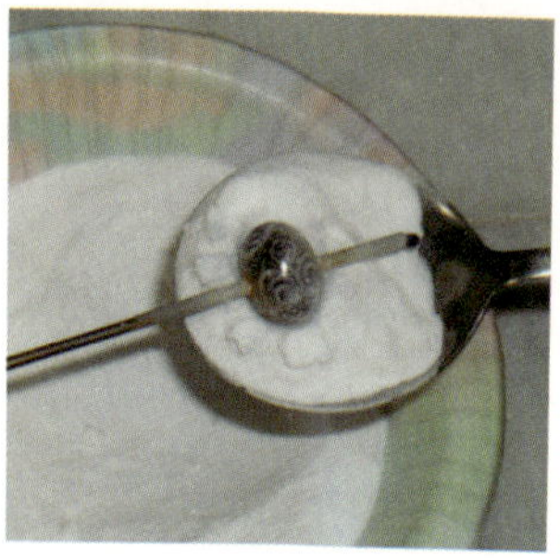

Diana starts by making a simple round bead, but does it in such a different way that I thought it warranted a little discussion. She first made a really big gather on the end of a transparent teal rod, as in the upper left photo. Then she lightly touches it to a warmed mandrel that she is rotating away from her. She winds it as a wide band but feeds it onto the mandrel over several rotations, as in the second photo. After she has wound sufficient glass onto the mandrel, she flame cuts the excess and rounds up the bead by heating the rotating glass in the flame, as in the center left photo. Once round she allows the bead to set up before decorating it.

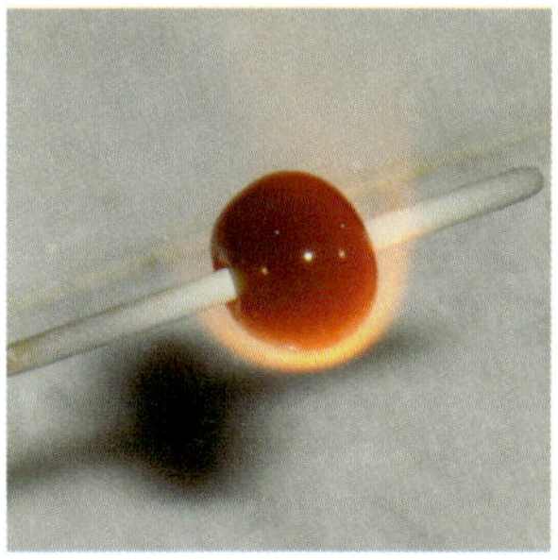

The decoration scheme for this bead is relatively simple. First Diana builds up two rings of four stacks of dots. Each stack consists of six alternating dots of white and blue glass of successively smaller diameters, as she is doing in the fourth photo on the left. In between the sets of paired stacks, she adds a smaller stack two dots high, as in the lower left photo. She melts all of these dots into the surface of the bead.

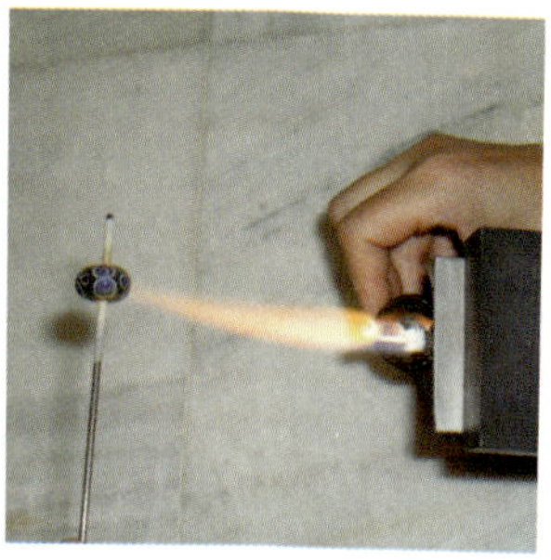

Next Diana works at making the bead look old. The first step of this process is to apply a light dusting of goldenrod enamel (#9250) to both ends of the bead, as in the upper right photo. You can see how little she has added by looking at the lower right photo. Then Diana uses baking soda to roughen the bead surface. She does this as before by rolling the bead in baking soda, as in the second photo on the right, and then immediately heating the bead in the flame, as in the center right photo. Notice how with this smaller bead she can just use a spoon to hold the baking soda.

The last step in making this bead look old is to apply a light fuming of silver to the surface. To do this Diana holds a small grain of fine silver balanced on a short quartz rod right at the tip of the inner flame, as in the fourth photo on the right. She uses a quartz rod because it will not soften in the flame and swallow the grain like borosilicate can. Notice that the flame used for fuming silver is a slightly reducing one, rich in propane. Also see how far out the bead is being held in the flame. If it gets too much closer it will burn off the silver as fast as it is applied. But if you do not keep the bead warm enough, the silver fume will not stick and can be rubbed right off of the bead. From here the bead goes right into the annealer. The finished bead can be seen in the lower right photo.

Ancient Melon Bead

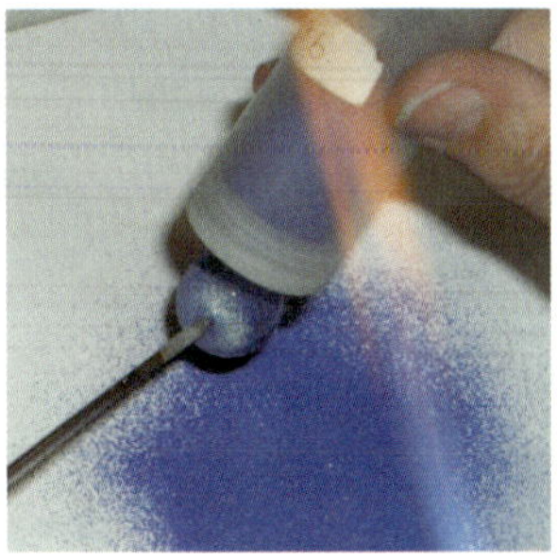

The last bead of the ancient series that Diana is going to demonstrate is what she calls an Ancient Melon Bead, because the indentations in the outer surface give it a melon-like appearance. Diana starts this bead using her usual construction techniques of first winding the bead to length with dark amber, as in the upper left photo, followed by the addition of extra glass to build up the profile of the bead. Because this bead is so short compared to most of her other beads in this booklet, this was one of the few times that the additional glass was added in the form of circumferential wraps.

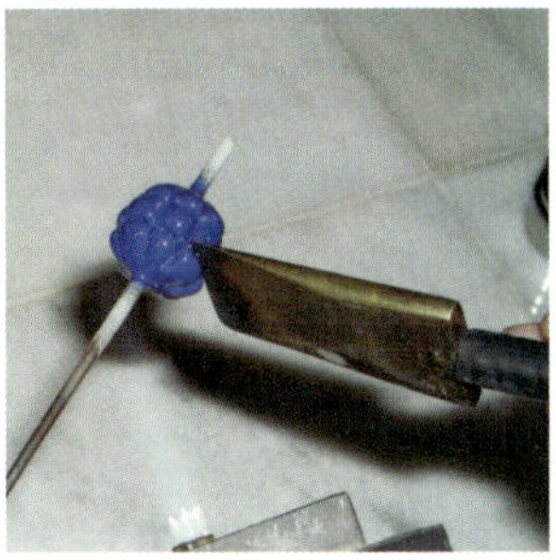

Now Diana coats the bead with a few layers of different colored enamels, each layer applied as a complete coating on the entire bead surface. Diana applies the enamel in her usual manner, shaking the color on from multiple directions. She applies them in the following order: goldenrod (#9250), aquamarine (#9550), white (#9010) and brilliant blue (#9660) as in the last three photos on the left and the first one on the right.

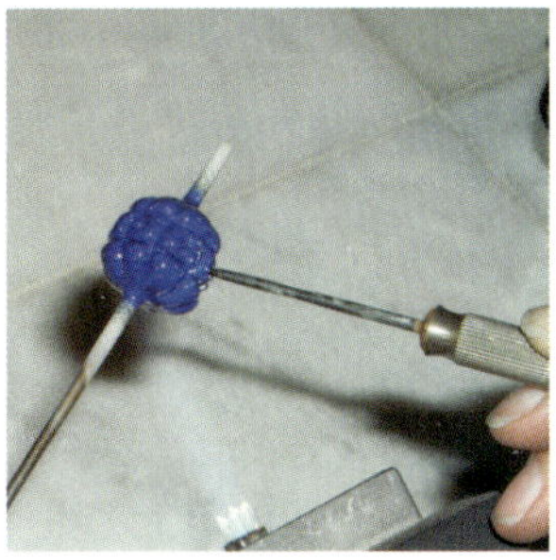

Next Diana distorts the surface of the bead to give it heavy texture, which will result in color variation in the final bead. As she sandblasts the bead in the final step, the valleys in the bead will be shielded from the abrasive cutting by the silicon carbide jet, producing interesting color variations. Diana adds two types of surface distortion to the bead. First, she puts both circumferential and end-to-end linear valleys into the surface by splashing heat onto the surface and pushing the sharp edge of her brass Stump shaper into it, as in the second photo on the right. Second, she adds point indentations into the center of each of the squares around the center of the bead that were formed by the linear indentations. She puts these indentations into the bead using a tungsten pick, as in the center right photo. With this the flameworking of the bead is done and she transfers the bead to her annealer to cool down.

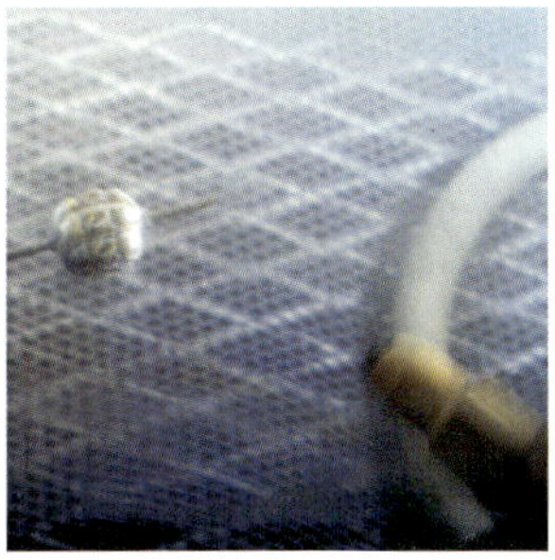

Diana then puts the bead, still on the mandrel but with release removed, into the sandbasting cabinet. She blasts it from multiple directions, purposely trying to get a variable etch, as in the fourth photo on the right. She blasts from each direction until she can just start to see the color of the base bead starting to show through. This insures that she gets the complete variation in color possible on the bead.

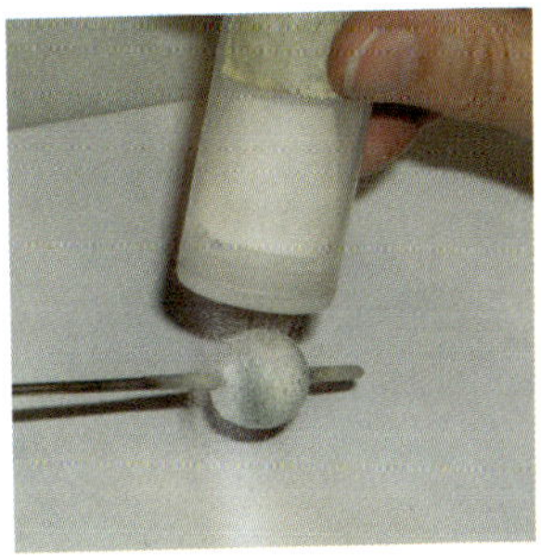

In the photo of the finished bead to the lower right you can see the color variation that she achieved. She blasted from the lower right of this side and cut all the way into the dark transparent amber base. To the left the yellow has been exposed. As you look down into the valleys you see transitions through the rest of the colors to the blue at the deepest points. She was very particular in her choice of enamel colors to get strong contrast between the layers.

Great Wave Bead

The next bead that Diana will make uses most of the techniques that she has demonstrated to this point, making it a very technically challenging bead. But aesthetically Diana is not as excited about it as her newer work because she is translating the ideas of another into a different media, glass. Her source for this design is "The Great Wave Off Kanagawa," by the great Japanese painter Katsushika Hokusai, pictured to the left. Even so it is a real work of art.

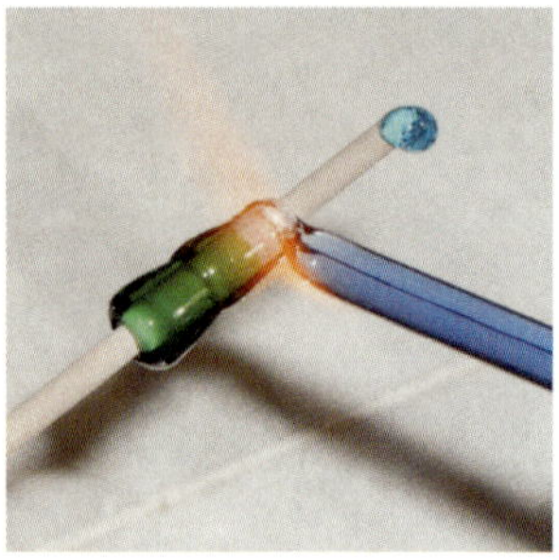

Diana starts by winding a base core bead of transparent aqua that transitions to medium transparent blue, as in the second photo to the left. She wound the first half in aqua, marvered it to a taper, and then overlapped the aqua in the tapered area with the blue. She stopped briefly, as in the center left photo, to see how much longer she had to make the bead to match the length of some dichroic pieces that she is going to add. She then finishes the bead to that length and shapes it into a nice bicone with her graphite paddle. If the ends get a little out of whack she can adjust them by pushing up on them with her graphite paddle, as in the fourth photo on the left.

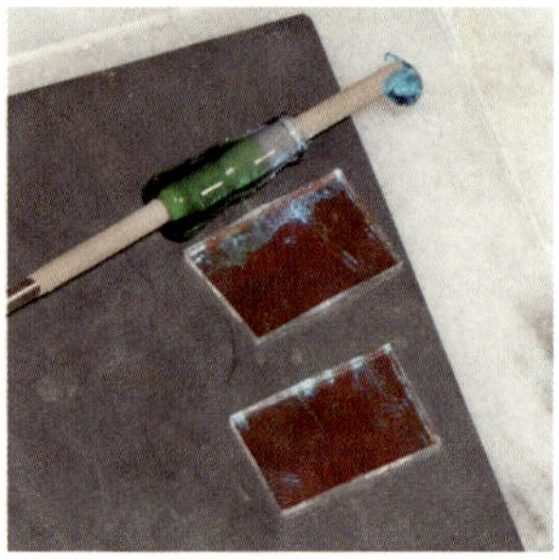

Diana next wraps the two pieces of dichroic glass onto the bicone, as she did for the Thought River Bead. She first warms the dichroic piece and centers it on the hot bead dichroic side down, as in the lower left photo, and then squeezes it down onto the core by pinching the bead and the dichroic glass together with her tweezers, as in the upper right photo. Using tweezers speeds the process of forming the dichroic glass around the bicone.

As the dichroic glass softens Diana continues to use her tweezers to bend and stretch it to fit and cover the base bead, as in the second photo on the right. She also ensures that all of the dichroic coating is well attached to the bead surface. She presses along the edges of the dichroic piece with the back of her tweezers to make sure that she has caused sufficient flow of the clear glass backing to cover the coating at the edges and especially the ends, as in the center right photo.

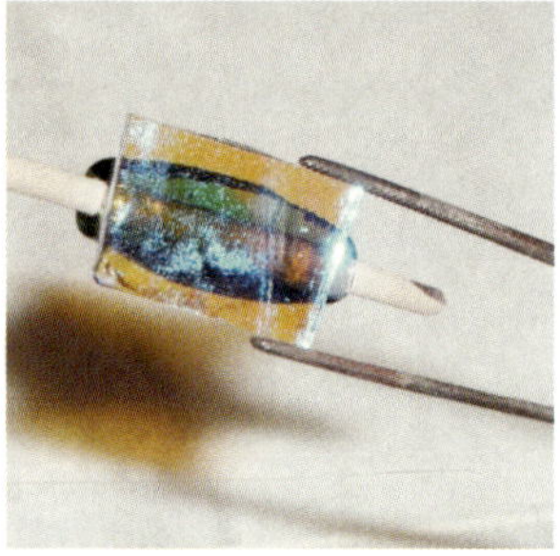

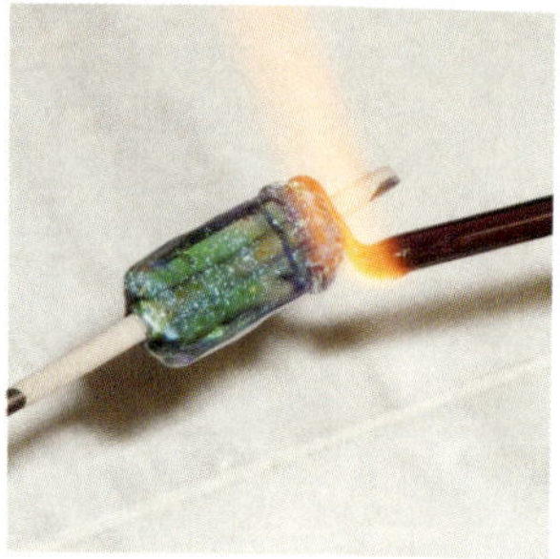

Diana adds a little more transparent blue to the top of the bead, as in the fourth photo on the right. Without this extra blue, the top of the sky would appear clear. In addition, to develop variation in the sky, she applies horizontal stripes of transparent amethyst at the top of the bead, as in the lower right photo and the upper left photo on the next page. She also applies transparent medium blue stringer for variation, as in the second photo on the next page.

Next Diana begins to shape the bead into her favorite oval lozenge shape. After starting she decides she wants to add a little extra thickness to the bead and applies more light

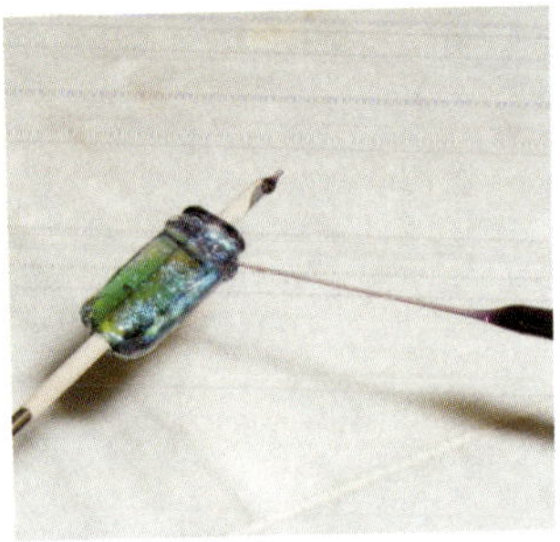

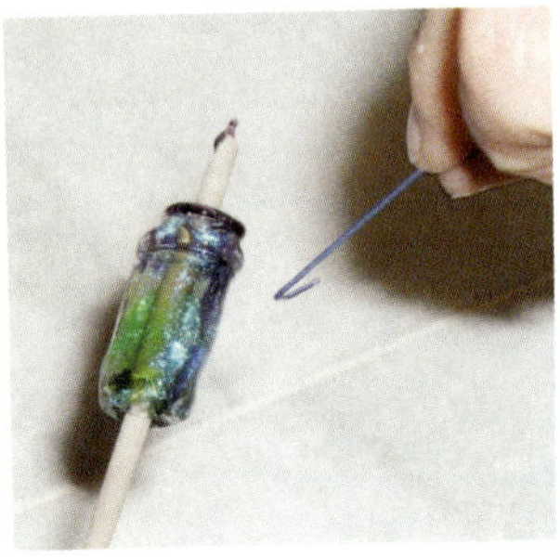

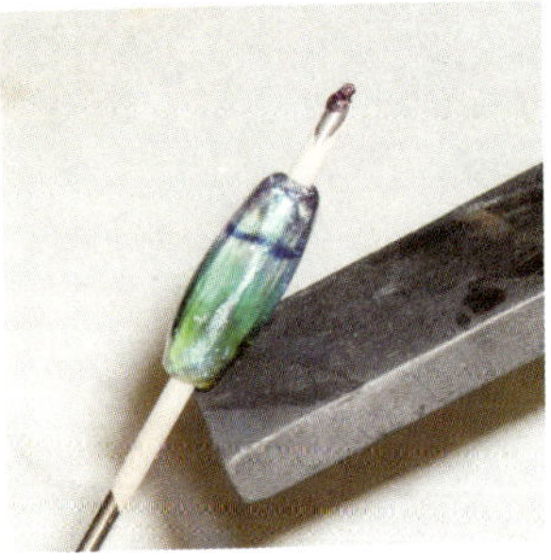

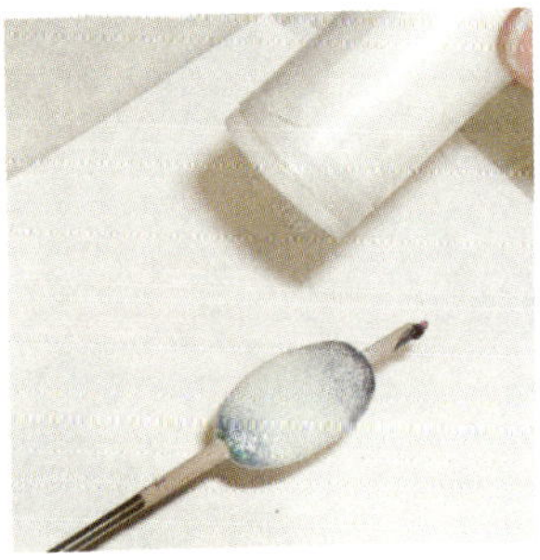

transparent blue to both faces, as in the center left photo. She finishes shaping the oval using the circular passes with her paddle, as in the fourth photo on the left.

Now it is time for Diana to apply enamel to the bead. None of these layers are intended to completely cover the bead. She first applies white (#9010), which she sprinkles on around the central section of the bead, as in the lower left photo. This layer will be exposed later to represent foam at the top of the waves. Next she applies a coating of aqua (#9050) on the bottom half of the bead, as in the upper right photo. She allows a light dusting of aqua to go up further for color variation at the top of the wave. Now she applies a light coating of brilliant blue (#9660) on the bottom third of the bead, as in the second photo on the right. She finishes with a light dusting of aqua just below center, as in the center right photo. This dusting gives the water a mottled look.

Next she finishes shaping the bead and smoothes the enamel coating with circular passes of her paddle, as in the fourth photo on the right. The variations in the colors of the coated surface can be seen in the last two photos on the right. Notice the variation in the enamel coloration, going from blue at the bottom to aqua in the middle to white at top. The last flameworking step is to fume the bead with gold and silver. Diana uses has the neat fuming kit seen in the upper left photo on the next page that can be purchased from JanHein van Stiphout. The two tools are appropriately color coded gold and silver. Each has a quartz rod mounted in it on which to put a grain of the pure metal when fuming. A cover that is not shown protects the rods and prevents loss of the metal when not in use. The cover also has a small chamber in which to store addition fine gold and silver casting grain for future use.

Fuming is a tricky process and some artists find it hard to control. Besides getting the metal grain in the right place to produce fumes, the artist has to also ensure that the bead is at the right temperature to allow the metal to bond to the surface. If the bead is too cold, the fumes will plate the glass but will not stick to it and can be rubbed right off. If the bead is too hot, the fumes will be burned off the bead as fast as it is applied.

I have seen two different methods used to ensure that the bead is at the right temperature to accept the fumes. The first method is to heat up the bead until it is lightly glowing and then take it out of the flame for six seconds before putting it in the back part of the flame and starting to fume. The second method is experimenting to find the sweet spot in the flame to bring the bead to the right temperature and holding it there to remain at that temperature. This method can be tricky because different torches and different flame adjustments can make finding the sweet spot hard to read,

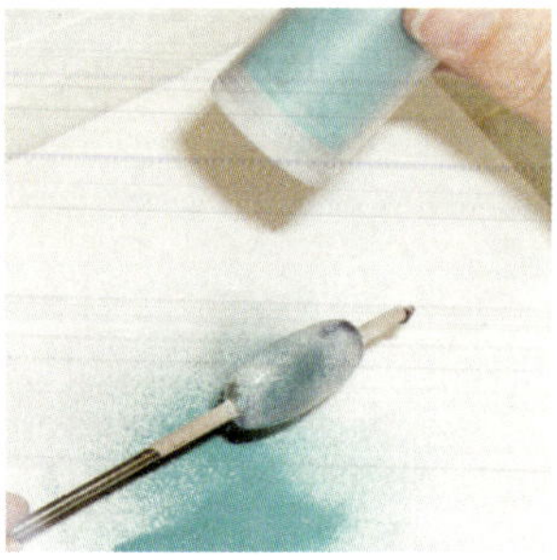

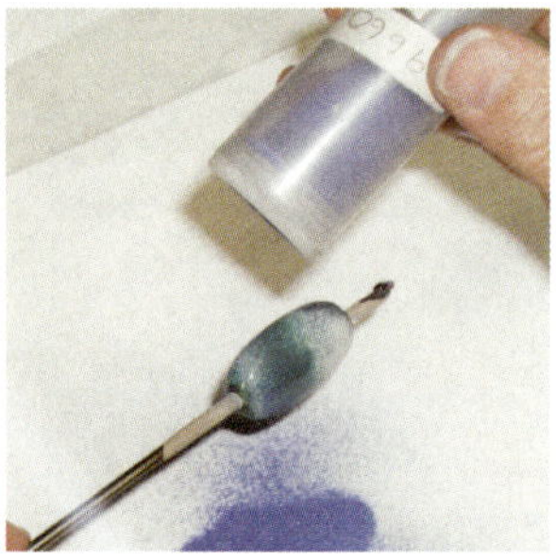

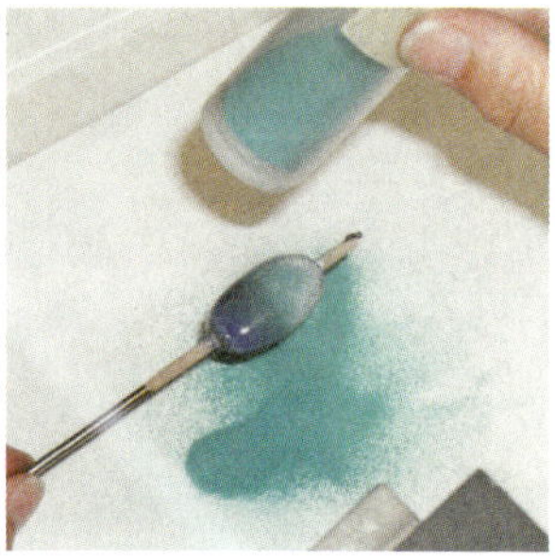

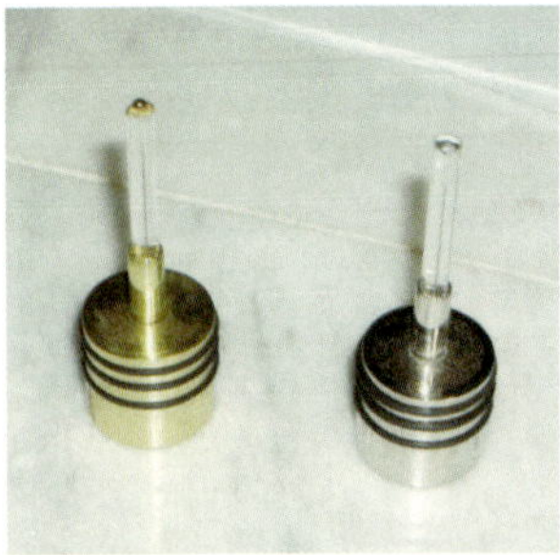

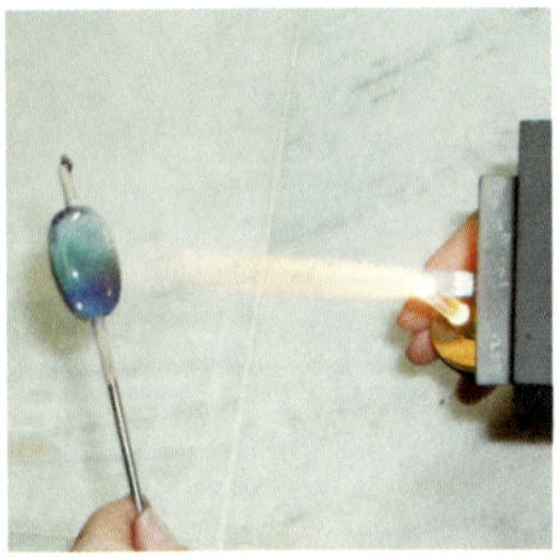

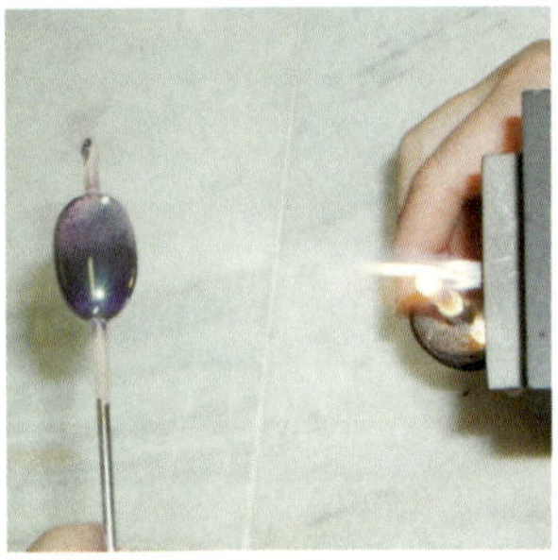

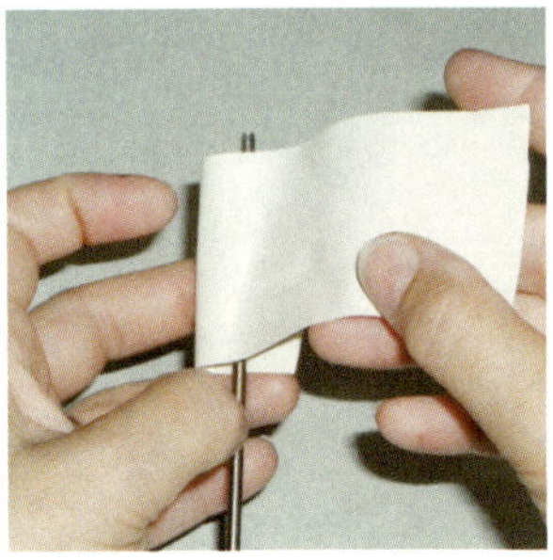

but this is the technique that Diana has mastered and uses in her work.

For this bead Diana applies a light fuming of gold followed by a light fuming of silver. The combination of the two develops a greenish color. In the second photo on the left Diana is applying the gold fume. If you look closely at the photo you see that the tongues at the front of the torch are short and equal in length. These are the characteristics of a slightly oxidizing flame and gold fuming is best applied with this type of flame. She is holding the gold in the flame just past the tips of the tongues and the bead out at the proper temperature spot.

Compare that photo to the third photo on the left. Here the tongues are longer and of unequal length with the center one being much longer. These are the characteristics of a slightly reducing flame, and this is the type of flame that is used for fuming silver. She holds the silver right in the longest tongue and the bead in the sweet spot. The fourth photo on the left shows the bead after the light fuming has been applied. You can see how the white has turned pink and there is a partial mirror finish on the surface. The bead is then put into the kiln and well annealed.

After the bead is cool Diana prepares it for sandblasting. For this bead she wants to precisely control what parts of the bead are etched so she uses resist to cover those areas that she does not want etched. The resist that she uses is a thick PVC tape about two inches wide. In the lower left photo she is wrapping a double layer around the circumference of the bead. She stretches and pushes down on the tape as she applies it to try to get it to conform to the bead surface as much as is possible. She tries to avoid trapping any air bubbles under the tape. These allow penetration of the tape by the silicon carbide and should be avoided.

The next step is drawing the image that she wants to sandblast into the bead on the resist. In this case she is drawing out a simplified version of the wave using a soft lead pencil, as in the upper right photo. Here is where the choice of resist can make a difference, as not all resists are easy to draw on. Diana now cuts the resist along the pattern lines. She uses a sharp scalpel to cut short sections at a time, as seen in the second photo on the right. She makes sure that she gets a continuous cut so that when she removes sections of the resist they come off easily and do not distort the image. If there are areas of the resist to be removed at different times, as in this bead, she still makes all the cuts now because after the first sandblast most of the pattern sketched on the resist will be lost.

Diana will blast the sky first, so she removes the resist off of the sky section of the bead. This exposes the outline of

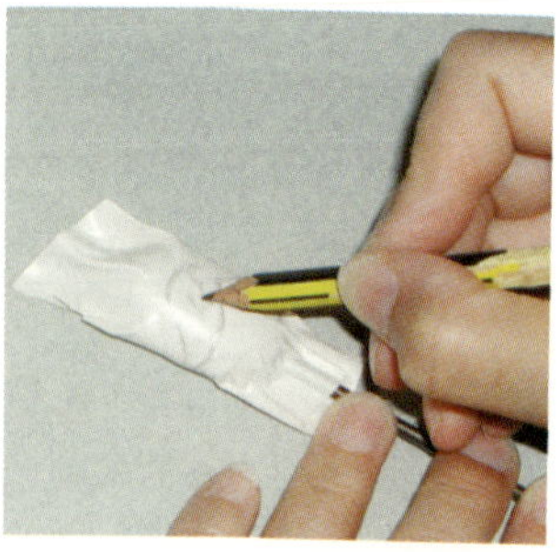

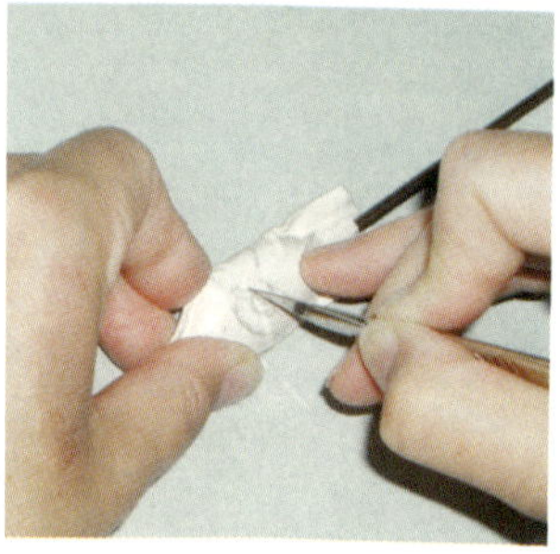

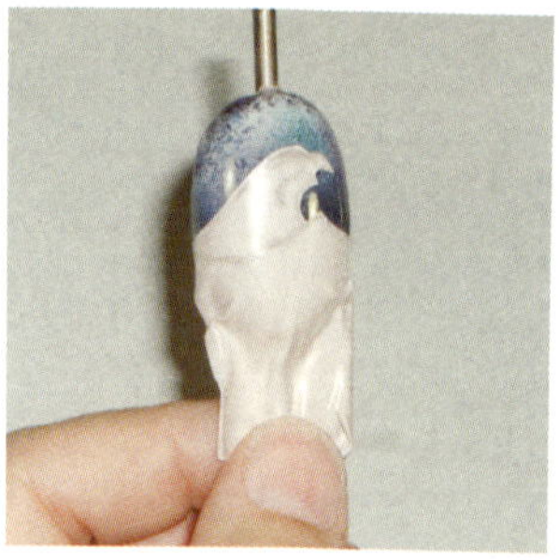

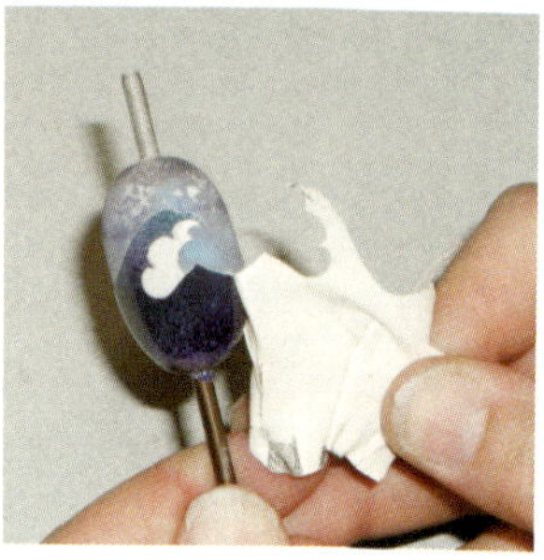

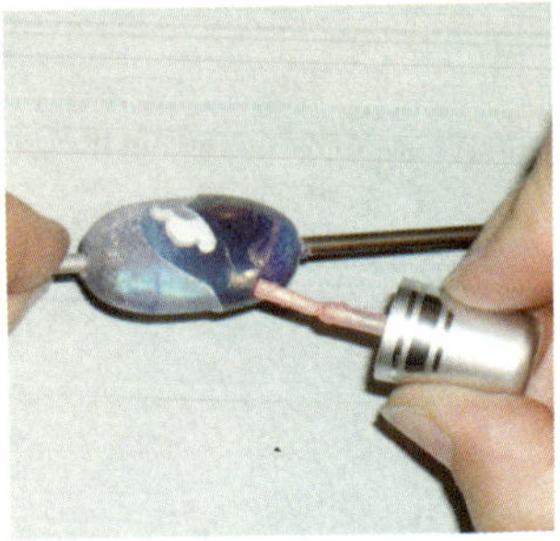
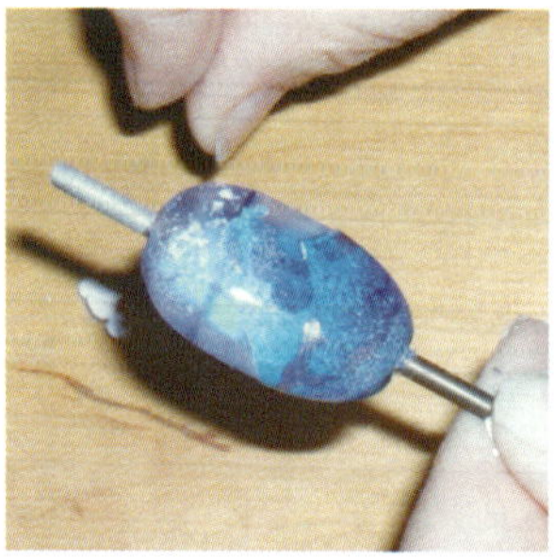

the wave, as in the center right photo. She then puts the bead into the cabinet and blasts the exposed section of the bead, as in the fourth photo on the right. She cuts through the fuming and most of the enamels almost to the base bead, leaving a little white to look like spray. After blasting the sky to her satisfaction she removes the resist off of the section that she will etch. Thus in the lower right photo on the previous page she is removing the resist from the ocean section of the bead, leaving a small section of resist on the underside of the wave. Diana will be using etching liquid to remove sections of the fuming from the ocean part of the bead. If she wanted to remove all of the fuming she could dip the bead as is into the etching liquid. But what she wants is a wave-like structure of fuming in this area, so she uses nail polish to paint wave-like images onto the bead. The nail polish will act as a resist to the etching, leaving fumed wave-like images on the ocean.

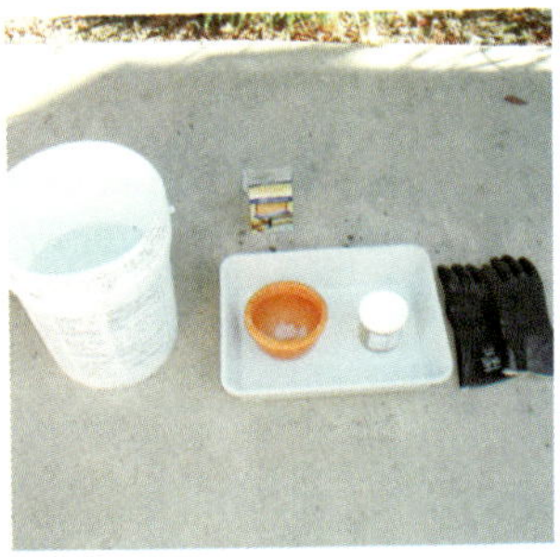
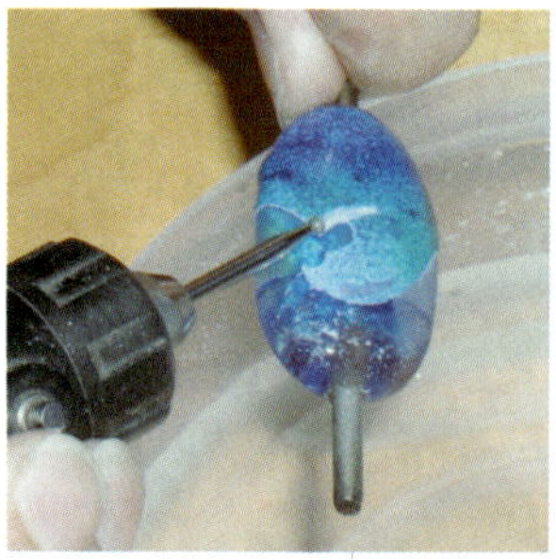

The second photo on the left shows the set up for using the etching liquid. Even though it is not as hazardous as hydrofluoric acid, you have to be careful with this stuff because it is poisonous and can cause chemical burns. You should wear splash goggles whenever using it. In addition, as you are opening the jar use heavy rubber gloves and a rubber apron. The setup from right to left consists of heavy rubber gloves, a cat box to catch any spillage, the plastic jar of etching liquid, a container with a mixture of baking soda and water, and last a large container of water. When opening the jar with your gloved hands take the lid off the jar with one hand while holding the jar down with the other. Never handle an open jar of etching liquid.

The exposed fuming is etched by dipping the bead on the mandrel into the etching liquid for about twenty seconds, as in the center left photo. The acid on the bead is then neutralized by dipping it into the baking soda solution until it stops bubbling, as in the next photo. Last the bead and mandrel are thoroughly rinsed by swishing the bead in the clear water. Never raise the bead above your hand until you have completed all three steps or you chance having etching liquid run down the mandrel onto your hand. The nail polish masking can then be removed by scraping it with your fingernail, as in the lower left photo or by using remover to reveal the bead seen in the upper right photo.

The image at this point is visible but Diana likes to accent it by using a rotary motor tool with a ball diamond bit, as in the center three photos on the right. The ground surface itself and exposure of some the white enamel beneath the surface forms the white foam on the wave and the smaller wavelets in the ocean. She dips the bead and the tip of the tool frequently into a dish of water as she grinds to lubricate the diamond bit and keep down the glass dust. The finished bead is shown in the photo to the right.

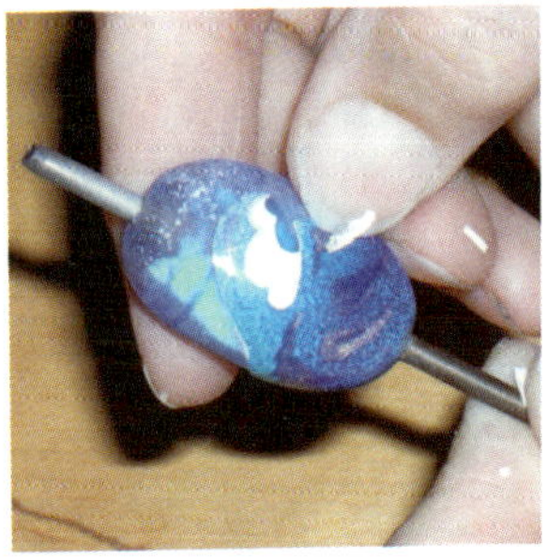

Cityscape Bead

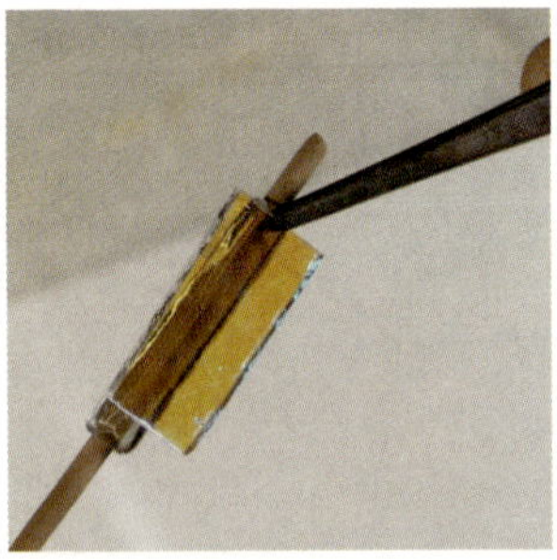

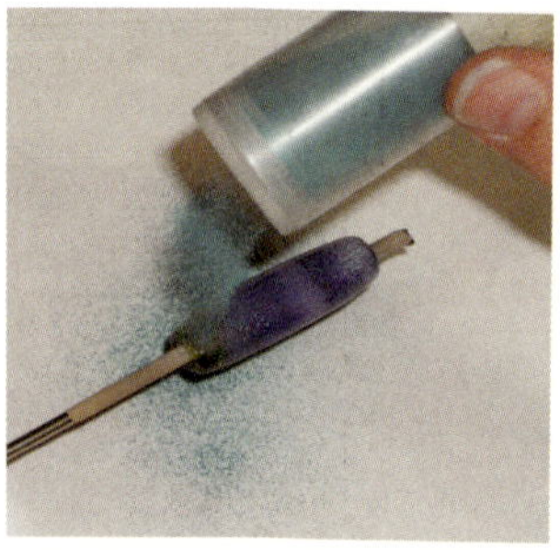

Our last bead demonstration is Diana's Cityscape Bead (her husband calls it a tourist bead). This bead demonstration uses most of the same steps from the last bead. The etching plans are more complicated here and Diana shows how to use multiple pieces of resist. Savor this last demonstration, it is a good one.

Diana starts this bead by winding a long clear base bead, which she covers with two pieces of dichroic glass that she applies dichroic side down, as in the upper left photo. As before the two pieces are applied to opposite sides of the bead and overlapped so that they cover the whole surface of the bead.

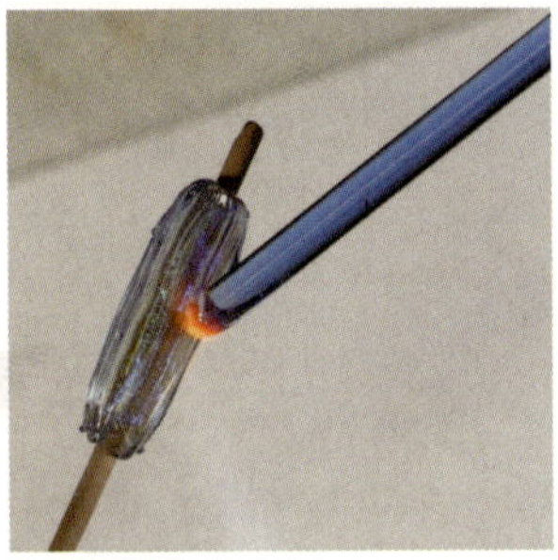

She then builds up the diameter and profile of the bead by adding lengthwise stripes of medium transparent blue glass, as in the second photo on the left. After this glass is smoothed and shaped, Diana wraps some stringer of transparent amethyst and dark transparent blue around the top half of the bead, as in the center left photo. These stringers help achieve color variation of what might be clouds in the sky.

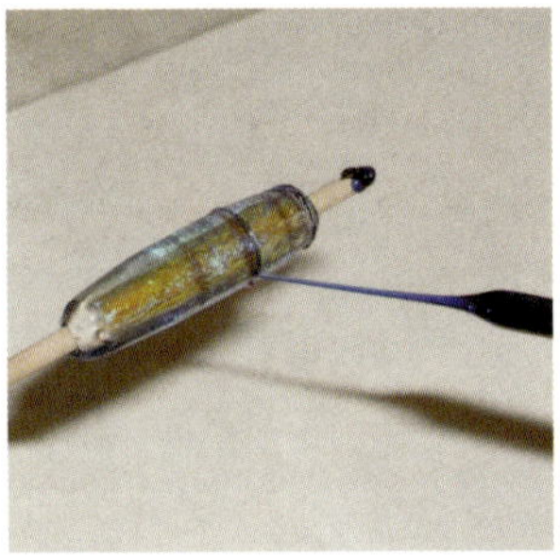

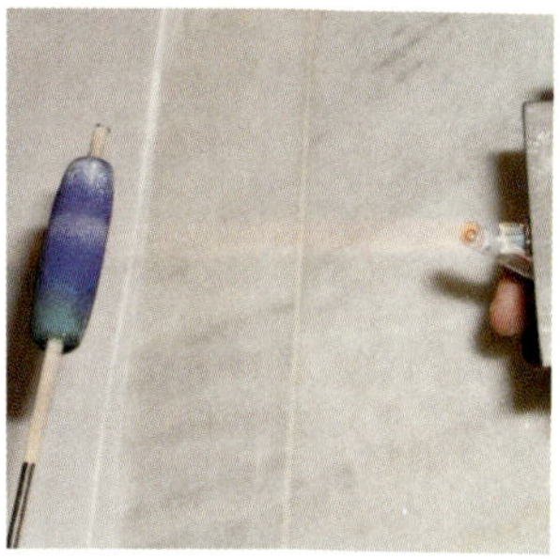

Next Diana applies enamels that will help give the skyscrapers and ground around them, which she will carve into the bead, a twilight appearance going from light to dark. These enamels are applied in the following order. First she adds a light dusting of white (#9010) to the top of the bead, and next adds a layer of new purple (#9740) to the middle of the top half of the bead, as in the fourth photo on the left. Then she applies a layer of brilliant blue (#9660) onto the middle of the bead, as in the lower left photo. Last she apples aquamarine (#9550) to the bottom of the bead, as in the upper right photo. The aqua at the bottom is there because this city is supposed to be situated on the seashore like Manhattan.

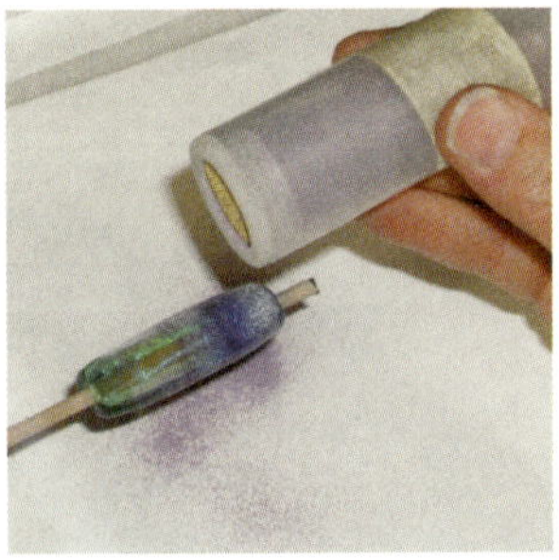

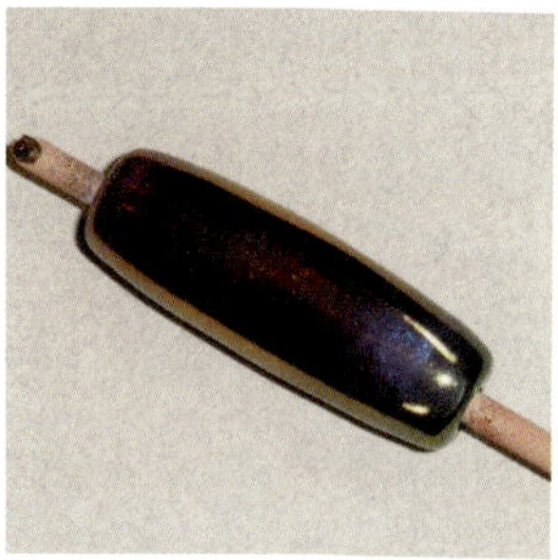

Diana then shapes the bead into the long lozenge shape that she likes so much. She starts by flattening it slightly by squashing it between her paddle and the mini-marver mounted on her torch. She follows this with circular passes of her paddle to smooth out and round the edges of the lozenge, as in the second photo on the right. In this photo you can also see the final enamel color scheme that was applied to the bead.

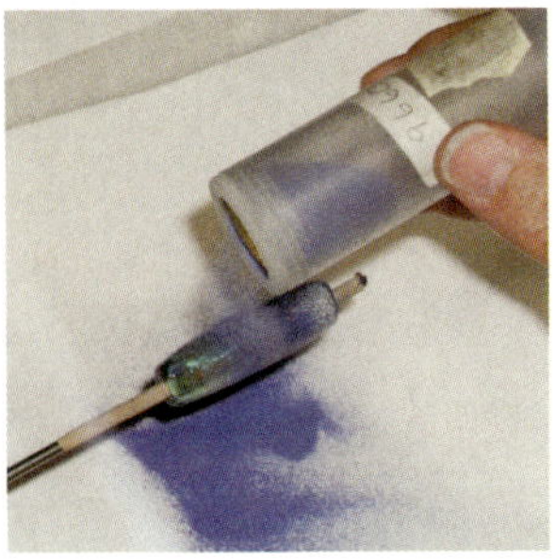

As in the wave bead, Diana next adds a light fuming of metallic gold over the entire enameled surface. Notice in the center right photo how she positions the gold casting grain just beyond the tongues in the flame. Also notice that the tongues are short and of the same length, indicating an oxidizing flame. Additionally, see how the bead is positioned in the sweet spot about five inches from the tip of the torch so that the the bead will be at just the right tempera-

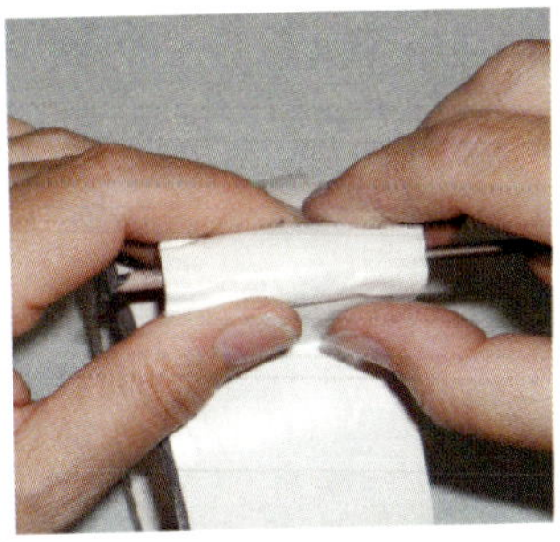
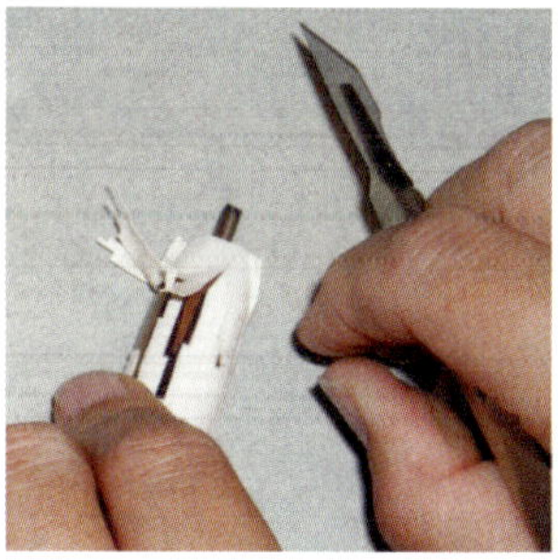

ture for the gold to stick to it. After fuming, the bead is put into the kiln to anneal. The fourth photo on the right of the previous page shows the fumed bead after it came out of the kiln.

Diana next prepares the bead for sandblasting. She cuts a three inch long section of the two-inch-wide, 5.5-mil-thick plastic tape that she uses for a resist, as in the lower right photo on the previous page. It is similar to 3M type 470 Electroplating tape, which is a 7.1-mil-thick vinyl tape available in widths of ¼, ½, ¾, 1, 1½, 2, 3, 4, 6, and 13 inches. She likes this tape because it sticks well and can be stretched to conform to the shape of the bead.

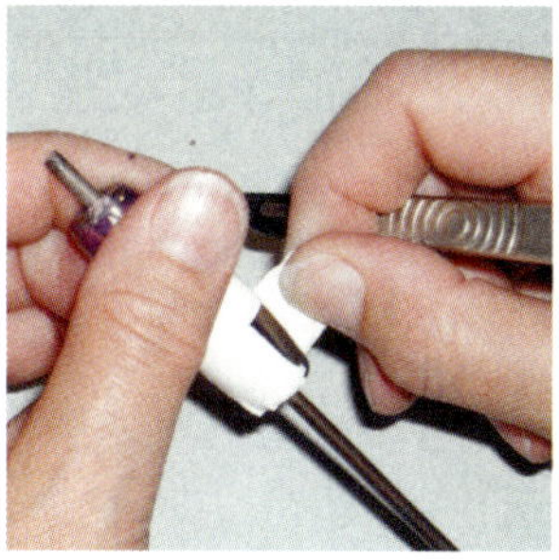

She rolls this tape around the circumference of the bead twice, making sure that it adheres well and does not trap any air bubbles underneath the tape, as in the upper left photo. She then plans out her etching strategy by drawing directly onto the resist with a soft lead pencil, as in the second photo on the left. The sketched etching plan of the building silhouettes can just barely be seen next to a finished bead in the center left photo.

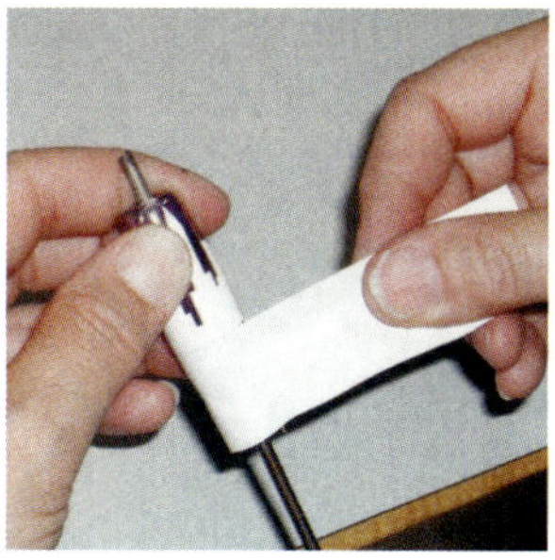

Diana then cuts out the sketched city skyline using a sharp scalpel, as in the fourth photo on the left. She takes great care to completely cut through all of the resist. She cuts short sections at a time, coming in from different directions, making sure that each section connects to the previous one, as in the fourth photo on the left. She doesn't want any stretching or distortion to occur from incomplete cuts when she removes it. As she cuts through the resist the scalpel will lose its edge as it is pulled across the hard bead surface. Diana sharpens the blade on a stone after each short cut, as in the lower left photo, because the glass quickly dulls it

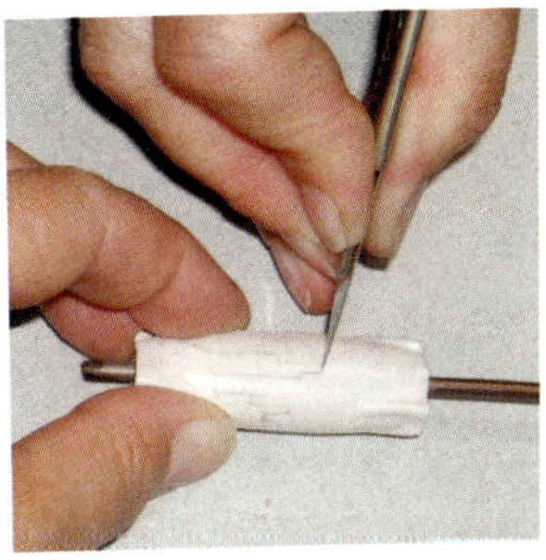
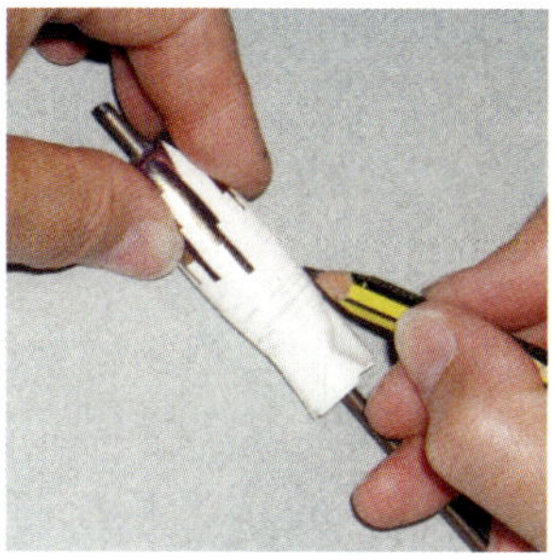

After she has cut the skyline into the sandblast resist, Diana removes the sky portion of the resist, as in the upper right photo. For a pattern with sharp internal corners like this one she also wants to make sure that she gets all the glue from the back of the resist out of the corners so it won't impede the etching.

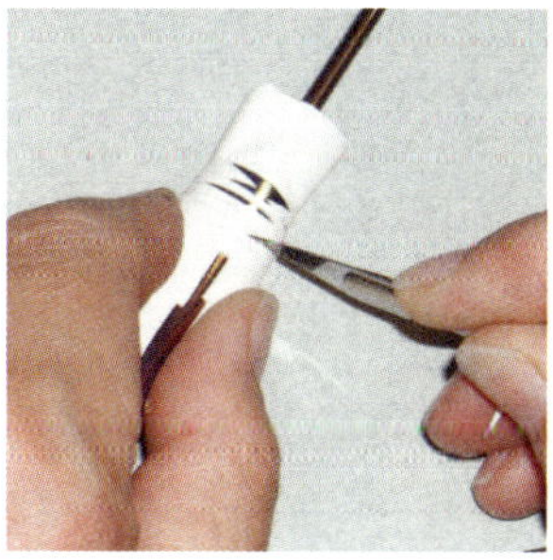

You may have noticed as Diana wrapped the resist onto the bead that it did not cover the ends very well. This does not matter at the top of the bead because she is going etch there, but it does matter at the bottom of the bead. She needs to add extra resist down there. She could just wrap a little more on the end but sealing the junction on the ruffled end can be difficult and risks opening up during blasting. So instead she goes up onto the bead where the resist is wrinkle free and trims off the skirt as in the second photo on the right. Then she adds a strip of resist wide enough to cover the end of the bead and allow a good seal at the bot-

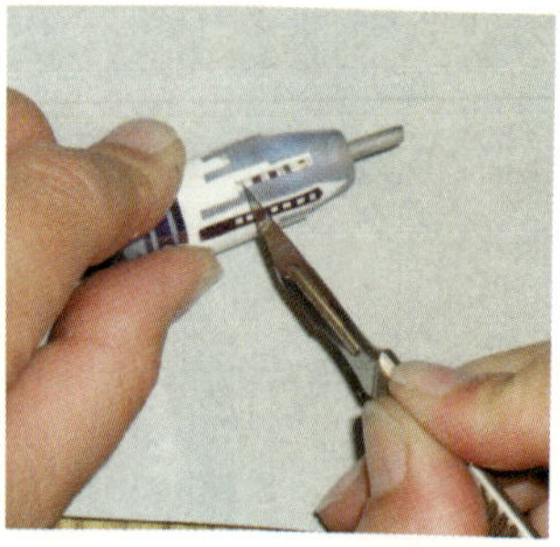

tom, as in the center right photo on the previous page.

Diana also wants to blast some ripples into the water on the lower part of the bead. So she sketches in the ripples onto the surface of the resist, as in the fourth photo on the right on the previous page, and then cuts them out, as in the lower right photo on the previous page. The masked blank, ready for sandblasting, is shown next to a finished bead in the photo to the left.

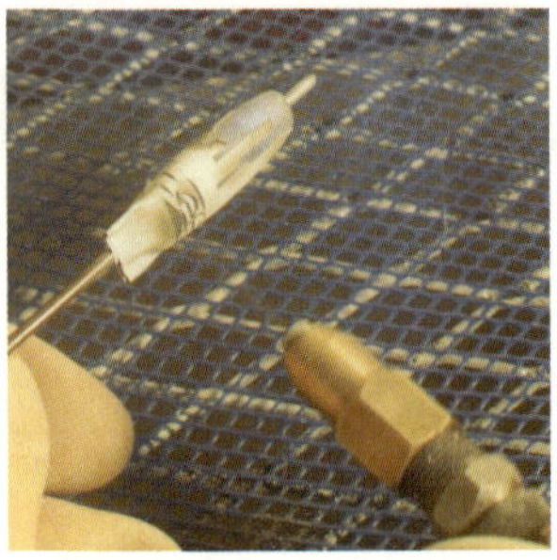

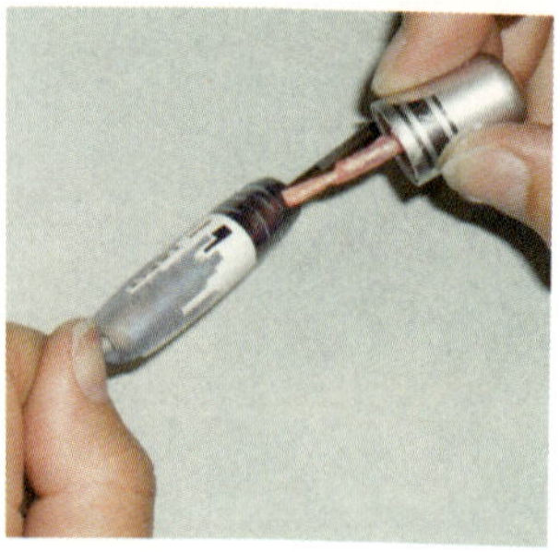

The bead is then put into the sandblast cabinet and blasted through the layers of enamel, as in the second photo on the left. With all the delicate cutouts this is where you really test how well your resist is attached to the bead. After blasting it is again time to prepare the bead for etching. Diana first removes all the resist from the lower half of the bead to expose the water area, as in the center left photo. Next she removes the upper of the two layers of resist on the top half of the bead, as in the fourth photo on the left. This leaves her an single layer of resist on which she can sketch out her detailed etching plan, as in the lower left photo.

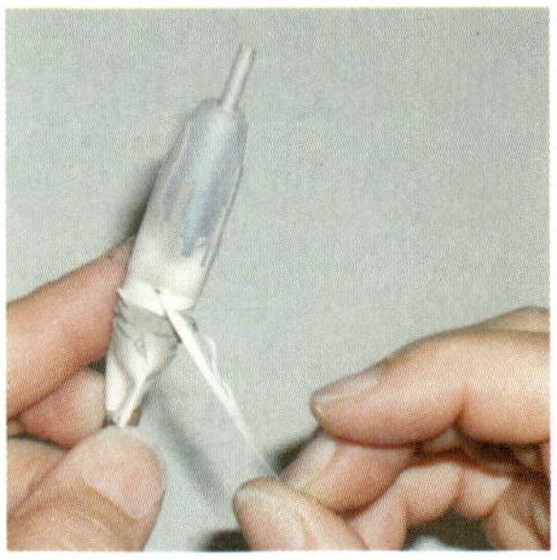

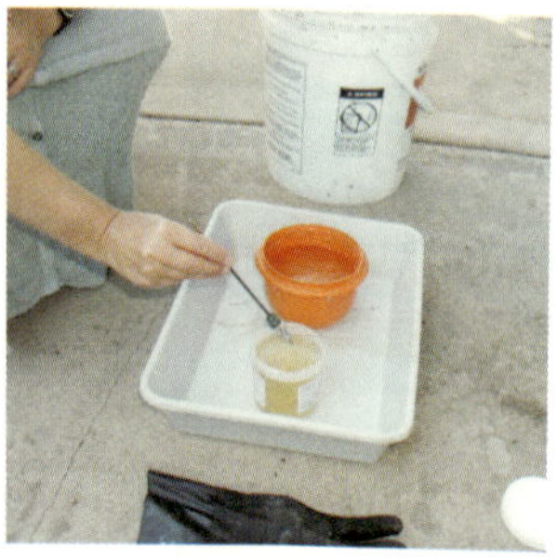

The top layer of resist was removed because it is hard to cut fine detail through more than one layer. Diana wants to use tape rather than fingernail polish as the resist on this portion of the bead because it will be easier to form the delicate design and sharp corners of the windows that she wants to etch into the gold fuming. These windows are visible in the upper right photo as she cuts the pattern for them out of the resist. Last Diana adds some wavelets using nail polish resist on the bottom half of the bead, as in the second photo on the right. This will be the only section of the water that will remain fumed.

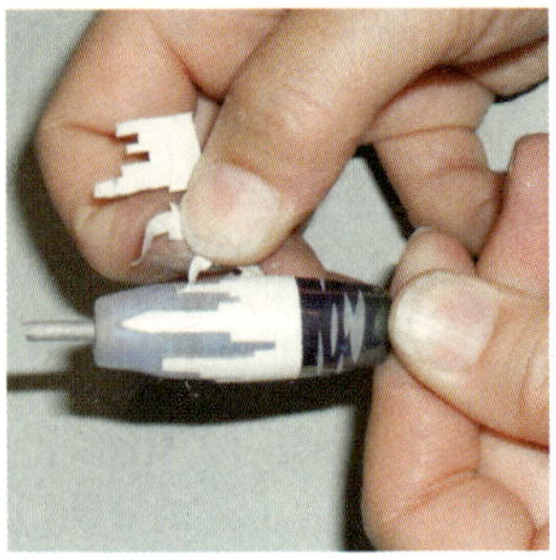

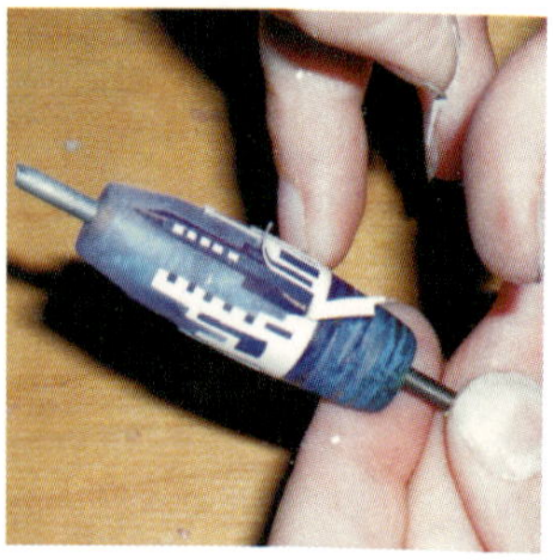

With that the bead is ready for acid etching. In the center right photo Diana is seen preparing to start the process by dipping the bead in the etching liquid. The process is basically the same as was done for the last bead. She first dips the bead into the etching liquid for about ten seconds to etch off the gold fuming, then she neutralizes the acid by dipping the bead into the baking soda solution, and finally she rinses off the bead in the clear water to remove the baking soda. If needed, multiple dip cycles or increased dip time can be used to get a greater degree of etching, but it will etch the glass matt. The same precautions for using the etching solution discussed before apply here also.

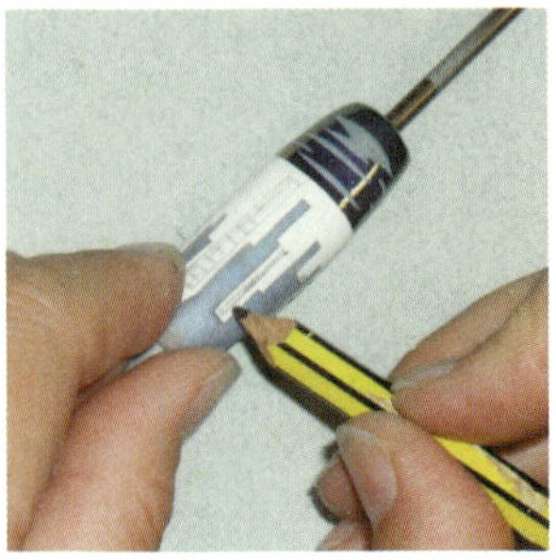

With this step done all that remains is to peal off the last of the tape resist, as in the fourth photo on the right, and remove the nail polish resist. Diana likes to scrape the polish off if she can. The finished bead is shown in the lower right photo. See the gold color of the twilight sunset glinting on the buildings and the light translucency in the sky.